environmental
education
in the
elementary school

environmental
education
in the
elementary school

LARRY L. SALE /
Gardner-Webb College
Boiling Springs, North Carolina

ERNEST W. LEE /
The University of North Carolina
at Greensboro

HOLT, RINEHART AND WINSTON, INC.
New York   Chicago   San Francisco   Atlanta
Dallas   Montreal   Toronto   London   Sydney

To Our Wives, Jan and Sue

foreword

In the early 1970s people in the United States quite suddenly awakened to the fact that the generally benign natural world in which they had been living was in danger of turning hostile. The danger was, of course, not inherent in the environment but had been created by man's neglect, abuse, and exploitation of the sick biosphere that he had inherited from his forebears.

At present we—and others around the world—are engaged in a great and promising effort to restore beauty, end the accumulation of toxic wastes, and reduce the potential threat of exponential population increase. This effort to make the world fit for the next generations to inherit depends upon more than sheer determination, however; it depends upon information and education as well.

In *Environmental Education in the Elementary School* Larry L. Sale and Ernest W. Lee have made a particularly important contribution. This book is not only filled with relevant factual information for teachers, but also emphasizes changes in education at the point at which they should begin if we are to protect and to preserve the biosphere: when ecological understanding and positive attitudes are developing in childhood.

Teachers will find that the authors have provided extensive, accurate, and well-documented material for use in the classroom. Equally important, the practical experience of the authors lends authority to the approaches that they suggest. Their book promises to fill a great and growing need for a new dimension in the education offered by our schools.

Harold G. Shane

Indiana University

vii

preface

Environmental Education in the Elementary School is a textbook intended to help teachers plan and implement environmental-education experiences for elementary-school children. It is designed to help teachers, either in service or in training, to analyze environmental problems and issues, to recognize basic concepts of ecology, to formulate curricula, and to devise appropriate instructional strategies. Prime emphasis is given to major ecological concepts and processes and a variety of instructional approaches to student investigations. Our intention is to provide teachers with a reservoir of relevant, practical, and valuable suggestions. Although the text has been prepared for teachers, reading it should be rewarding for anyone concerned about man's interaction with his environment.

The roots of our ecological crisis are associated with three broad but interrelated areas: overpopulation, poor conservation practices, and pollution. The major immediate problem, however, is man's ignorance of ecological concepts and processes, his insensitivity to his environment, and his failure to act positively in relation to it.

Man's relation to his environment has become one of the more complex questions of modern society. The magnitude of water and air pollution, "garbaged" landscape, and the disappearance of wildlife and natural vegetation seems overwhelming. Most of these problems can be attributed to man's ignorance and unconcern about the quality of his environment. Will future generations continue this disregard for the quality of their environment? What is the responsibility of the elementary school for environmental education? How can we develop citizens who will contribute to improvement of the quality of the environment?

The major theme of this book is a dual one: First, training concerned citizens who can contribute to environmental quality is a major function of our schools, and, second, it is imperative that this process begin during the formative years in elementary school. The text emphasizes an interdisciplinary approach, involving both the natural and social sciences. Understanding basic principles and concepts of ecology is not enough; we must help pupils to develop an appreciation of their environment and a value system that will guide positive action.

Part One, "Foundations of Environmental Education," provides a careful analysis of major environmental problems and issues, basic concepts and processes of ecology, appropriate instructional strategies, and approaches to designing the environmental-education curriculum.

Part Two, "Areas of Instruction," presents an introduction to selected subject matter and suggests how to involve students in learning experiences. Particular attention is given to concepts and processes and a wide variety of possible investigations for students.

The all-inclusive nature of environmental education has necessitated selecting only certain areas for emphasis. Many topics that might be incorporated into a school's environmental-education curriculum have not been treated: for instance, some aspects of health and nutrition and radiation pollution. The topics included were selected for their importance and because the information available offers a basis for pursuit of broader study of environmental problems.

Part Three, "Challenge for Survival," includes some practical ideas for providing teaching programs that will facilitate development of appropriate concepts and positive attitudes in pupils. Specific attention is given to the challenge facing us both now and in the future. A glossary of environmental terms and a resource guide for environmental education in the elementary school have been included.

To our knowledge, there is no other available textbook that focuses specifically on planning and teaching environmental education in the elementary school. This book is an attempt to help fill that void. From Chapter 1 the reader is invited to become an inquirer, to open his mind, to search for ideas beyond those in this book. If he is motivated to plan and provide satisfying environmental-education experiences for children and if this book provides him with valuable assistance, our efforts will not have been in vain.

We wish to express our appreciation to Harold Shane, who has offered innumerable suggestions, constructive criticisms, and major insights. For evaluative feedback on individual chapters we owe gratitude to our students and colleagues at the University of North Carolina at Greensboro. And sincere appreciation is owing to Jan Sale and Susan Hall for their assistance in the preparation of the manuscript.

Larry L. Sale
Ernest W. Lee

February 1972

contents

*environmental
education
in the
elementary school*

part one / **foundations of environmental education**

chapter 1 / understanding environmental problems and issues

The quality of the environment has become a major concern in the United States. The magnitude of the pollution problem was noted in detail by Rachel Carson in *Silent Spring* as early as 1962. Only in recent months, however, has the public become acutely aware of the severity of environmental deterioration. We are involved in a crisis! How have we ourselves contributed to bringing it about? Is it too late for solution? Historically, hostility toward the environment in the United States has prevailed. The early settlers found the rich wilderness hostile to their efforts to tame it. Today our environment is impoverished and crowded, reflecting man's failure to understand and respect basic ecological concepts and processes.

    •   Interest in this problem has exploded as individuals have learned that life on this planet is at stake. Scientists have predicted that, unless effective action is taken, by 1980 city dwellers will have to wear gas masks to survive air pollution and that air pollution and temperature inversion combined will nevertheless kill many people in some American cities; that by 1985 air pollution will have reduced by half the amount of sunlight that reaches the earth; that in the 1980s new diseases will reach plague proportions as a result of breakdowns in the major ecological system; that the earth's temperature will be significantly affected by increased carbon dioxide in the atmosphere, resulting in mass flooding, caused by the melting of polar ice caps, and other difficulties; that rising noise levels will cause sharp increases in heart disease and hearing disorders; and that collection of residual DDT in the human liver will seriously harm human health (Pekkanen, 1970). Current data indicate that air pollution is the most immediate threat to human survival. Resolution of this environmental crisis requires ecological analysis and positive action. Are we aware of the major environmental problems in our own communities? What are their major causes? What are we doing to find solutions?

IDENTIFYING MAJOR CAUSES
OF THE ENVIRONMENTAL CRISIS

The ecology issue is as insistent as the environmental destruction all around us: the smog that irritates our eyes, the pesticide-infested foods that we are afraid to eat, the polluted rivers and lakes that are no longer suitable for recreation and wildlife. We must recognize that the resources of the earth are finite. The intertwined roots of the ecological crisis are overpopulation, poor conservation practices, and pollution. Perhaps the foremost of these three is overpopulation.

Overpopulation

According to Ehrlich, the world's population of 500 million in 1650 had doubled to 1 billion by 1850, had doubled again to 2 billion by 1930, and now appears to be doubling every thirty-five years. At this rate, by the year 2000 there will be more than 7.5 billion people living on our planet. The world population is growing at the rate of 2 percent a year; theoretically in another thousand years each of us could have 300 million living descendants!

One of the most pressing concerns generated by this expanding population is food supply. Many people are already predicting world famine in the last quarter of this century. In fact, some individuals expect it in this decade. It is becoming increasingly apparent that something must be done both about population growth itself and about food supplies.

One new phenomenon relative to population growth in America is that we are not reproducing as rapidly as before; yet individuals are living longer. Average life expectancy among the ancient Romans was approximately thirty-five years. They had a very high infant-mortality rate. The life expectancy of the average modern American is increasing, however. Many experts insist that, if we cannot allow people to die, then we must sharply reduce the birth rate. If positive means like planned parenthood are not enough, then we may well have to resort, in the near future, to rather drastic measures like putting sterilization agents in the water supply or using antimeiosis drugs to curb the birth rate. These practices could have negative effects upon the consumer. There is a need for additional research relative to various sterilization controls.

Everett's account (1967) of one American's posterity is most informative. John Ely Miller died in a rambling farmhouse near Middlefield,

Ohio, at the age of ninety-five with perhaps the largest number of living descendants that any American has ever had. His survivors, in addition to 5 children, included 61 grandchildren, 338 great-grandchildren, and 6 great-great-grandchildren: a total of 410 descendants. John Miller's family illustrates a major fact of twentieth-century life: A majority of children become adults and have families of their own, mainly as a result of improved diet and medical care. Before this century malnutrition and disease played significant roles in curbing population growth. The progressive rate of increase is now so great that, had John Miller lived another decade, he might have left at least 1,000 living descendants.

If the present rate of population growth continues, then, the world may experience a severe famine within the next decade (Paddock, 1967). For the period 1965–1975 the United Nations projected population growth and corresponding food requirements for certain parts of the world (see Table 1.1). It is clear from careful study of Table 1.1 that, simply in order to maintain the inadequate dietary levels of 1965, the hungry nations would have to have increased their food production by 26 percent in a single decade. And the difficulties that prevent them from feeding their people today will be much greater tomorrow. Many parts of India, Pakistan, and China are experiencing famine today. Experts expect many other areas to experience famine during the last quarter of this century.

Can the moon serve as a safety valve for the earth's population? This "dead-end" philosophy relative to population development has serious inadequacies. There are too many unanswered questions concerning travel, development, and life support on the moon. However, even if all the information relevant to populating the moon were positive, man would need to change his behavior significantly, or the result on the moon would be basically the same as on earth.

Table 1.1 Future Food Requirements of the Hungry World*

	Population at Current Rates of Growth		Additional Food Production Needed Within 10 Years
	1965	*1975*	
East Asia	867 million	1.04 billion	20%
South Asia	975 million	1.25 billion	28%
Africa	311 million	404 million	30%
Latin America	248 million	335 million	35%
Total	2.4 billion	3.04 billion	26%

* From William and Paul Paddock, *Famine—1975! America's Decision: Who Will Survive?* (Boston: Little, Brown and Company, 1967). Copyright © 1967 by William and Paul Paddock. Reprinted by permission of Little, Brown and Company and Weidenfeld & Nicolson Ltd.

Poor Conservation Practices

Because of greed, waste, and the needs of an expanding population, vast areas of natural land are being spoiled and their plant and animal populations decimated. Poor planning has resulted in the indiscriminate exploitation of land, regardless of its potential agricultural use or its unique scientific or aesthetic value. Excessive strip mining is cutting ugly scars across the American landscape. This rape of the land has caused acute concern about adequate supplies of oxygen. We cannot afford to give up a million acres of photosynthesizing (oxygen-producing) vegetation each year, especially to pavements and factories that consume more oxygen. In time man may encroach on his "greenery" to such an extent that he will eliminate his major source of oxygen. Anyone who has breathed the air in a desert after that of a forest may have some inkling of what it will be like to wear an oxygen mask. As a result of poor management of water resources, the quality of our water continuously deteriorates. The number of animals classified as endangered species (becoming extinct) increases annually.

Pollution

Largely as a result of ignorance but also partly through greed and unconcern, we have perpetrated pollution that is quickly rendering our environment intolerable. Almost every major river system in the United States is polluted and has been for years. Rivers are poisoned by various man-made toxins: mining and manufacturing acids, oils, inorganic chemicals, and municipal sewage. The air is continuously polluted with by-products from internal-combustion engines. Approximately 100,000 tons of sulfur dioxide are released from chimneys in this country every day. Ninety million automobiles daily add a quarter million tons of carbon monoxide to the atmosphere. Other toxic gases emitted daily in lethal concentrations include various hydrocarbons, ozones, nitrogen dioxide, and hydrogen cyanide, to name only a few. Perhaps the most startling result of our advanced industrialization is the tremendous accumulation of carbon dioxide in the atmosphere. Excessive amounts of carbon dioxide in the atmosphere can cause the earth's temperature to rise significantly. If the temperature were to rise severely, polar ice caps could melt, resulting in rising ocean levels. The end result could be inundation of most coastal cities and deaths from heat—an earthly hell! (Marine, 1969, p. 28)

PROPOSED SOLUTIONS

Early in life we all become aware of our surroundings, long before we can pronounce such terms as "temperature," "wind," and "pollution." In early childhood we become aware of both living and nonliving components of our environment. Later we learn that man can change his environment. In recent years man has significantly changed his environment, but in many instances the results have been very negative.

As we are capable of changing our environment yet are at the mercy of the changes, a more thorough understanding and appreciation of basic ecological concepts could alleviate possible future environmental problems. These basic concepts are connected with basic social-science concepts, particularly those of sociology and anthropology. An interdisciplinary approach is desirable because man needs to understand better his interrelations with various components of his environment. According to social anthropologist Luther Gerlach, the real "movement," or "revolution," of today involves changing attitudes and values so that man will recognize himself as interdependent with, rather than plundering master of, his environment (Pekkanen, 1970).

Environmental Bill of Rights

Noted conservationist Paul F. Brandwein has developed an "environmental bill of rights," consisting of thirteen propositions reflecting his analysis of Western man's behavior toward his environment:

1. The present million or so species of organisms, including man, have come out of a history traversing several billion years—presumably from one primitive organism.
2. The environment available to organisms is limited; further for any species, the organism is adapted to a special environment and serves a special ecological niche. (In all probability, no two species occupy the same ecological niche.)
3. The environment is finite, species have particular adaptations, yet the growth of a population is held in natural checks by various combinations of starvation, disease, predation, and conflict.
4. Man, as dominant, has conquered or is on the road to conquest of his natural predators—and of disease.
5. Reproduction of organisms proceeds geometrically—so too the reproduction of man.
6. The problem of increase in population cannot be solved by increases in the production of food.
7. Biological evolution is the transmission of genes or DNA. For man this is no longer in effect. Instead what operates is cultural evolution, the transmission and transmutation of knowledge and values.

8. Natural and cultural selection together determine which species shall survive.

9. There is some reason to speculate that the small colony of "Homo recens" may escape the solar system in the distant future.

10. The concepts and values man accepts and imposes on his behavior function critically in the natural and cultural selection of which living things shall survive—this includes man himself.

11. The rational and hopeful solution is that man may seek a culture relevant to the modern century, make technology servant instead of master, control his population, and develop the factors which make his environment sanative—and fit for all life.

12. There is still time to develop a sanative environment. But the data—population data, resource data—indicate that time, like all our resources, is in short supply.

13. Therefore, it seems we have reached a cultural and biological point of no return. Therefore, the time to press for an enforceable Environmental Bill of Rights is now—irrevocably now. (Brandwein, 1970)

In applying these propositions, we educators should seriously consider what kind of a world we want for our children. It is our responsibility to help find answers to this question.

Never before has there been so great a need for efforts to preserve natural life on this planet. This need results from severe air and water pollution, misuse of natural resources, the gradual extinction of some living species, and wanton destruction of other living things. Man has already begun to feel the effects of this abuse on his own comfort and health. Furthermore, the balance of nature is being upset in unpredictable ways, and the potential consequences are alarming. The problem of preserving the environment is complicated by the increasingly technological character of our society and the rapidly growing world population. Conservation is no longer a local concern but rather a global problem directly affecting this entire generation and those to come. Many professional organizations in education are beginning to recognize the severity of the problem and to take some forcible action. The Association for Supervision and Curriculum Development published its resolutions for 1970–1971:

1. A.S.C.D. encouraged legislation to improve the quality of the environment.

2. A.S.C.D. supported needed financial aid for educational programs on the quality of the environment, which will lead to

environmental awareness, provide for an understanding of man's relationship to his environment, and promote a sense of responsible environmental stewardship.

3. A.S.C.D. declared that state boards of education should initiate and develop programs in environmental education that use environmental resources as study areas.
4. A.S.C.D. encouraged the development of environmental-education curricula and of appropriate instructional materials for continuing school programs.
5. A.S.C.D. endorsed and encouraged significant involvement of the nation's youth in the planning and development of environmental-education curricula and materials in order to promote both individual and collective responsibility for preservation of the natural environment. (*A.S.C.D. Resolutions*, 1970)

Thomas Carlyle said to an American friend, about a century ago, "You won't have any trouble in your country as long as you have few people and much land, but when you have many people and little land, your trials will begin" (Ingraham, 1967).

People and their activities create environments that threaten to destroy us all. We are rapidly building a world that is more than the body, mind, or spirit can bear.

Approaches to Environmental Legislation

Ehrlich (1967) has proposed some rather drastic steps that the United States might take toward a solution to the problems of population and food supply. The first is to establish a Federal population commission with a large budget for propaganda to encourage "reproductive responsibility." This commission would be charged with making clear the connection between the rising population and the declining quality of life. The second step would be to change American tax laws to discourage, rather than to encourage, reproduction. Ehrlich has suggested that those who "impose" children on society should be made to pay for the privilege, whenever they are able. The income-tax system would eliminate deductions for children and replace them with a graduated scale of tax increases for each additional child. A major problem relative to Ehrlich's proposal is that those who tend to have the larger families are not economically able to pay a tax anyway. The major thrust of this proposal is to make the American population socially responsible for its own increase.

The third proposal is for Federal laws making instruction in birth-control methods mandatory in the public schools. The fourth is to change the pattern of Federal support of biomedical research to emphasize broad areas of population regulation, environmental science, behavioral science, and disease prevention and control.

An essential question, according to Ehrlich, is that of quantity versus quality. He has argued that, if we cannot learn to curb quantity, then quality will be beyond our reach in any case. He has proposed that the United States should refuse to ship food to countries that are not making maximum efforts to limit their populations; assist other countries in the technology of population control; assist other countries to increase their yields on land cultivation; and use its power and prestige to press for global solutions to world population problems. All these points have validity; however, the refusal of food to hungry children has serious moral and political implications.

The very comprehensive Tukey report of 1965 offered 104 recommendations for principles, actions, coordination and systems studies, base-line-measurement programs, development and demonstration, research, and manpower relative to the pollution problem (President's Scientific Advisory Committee, 1965).

Carson (1962) expressed some very grave reservations about the use of chemical insecticides in our environment. She argued that we have put poisonous and biologically potent chemicals indiscriminately into the hands of people wholly or largely ignorant of their potential for harm. We are caught in a spiral in which insects have constantly evolved "super races" immune to particular insecticides, so that more and more deadly ones must be developed.

David M. Gates, a physicist turned botanist, has argued (1968) that man cannot survive on earth five more generations unless he changes his attitudes toward the natural world that supports him. Gates fears that the United States may go down in history as a sophisticated technological society that underwent biological disintegration through lack of ecological understanding. Professional educators, scientists, and public-service administrators must recognize the chasms currently separating science, technology, and public policy from the understanding of consuming citizens. The necessity for creating public and professional awareness of the problems of human ecology is of the first magnitude. We need a nationwide effort to create a concept of ecological citizenship, an effort that should be actively furthered by government and private sectors, by professional and lay groups, and by individual citizen consumers at all levels of our society: local, regional, state, and national.

White (1967) has pointed out that the recorded history of ecological change is still so rudimentary that we know little about what really has happened and what the results have been. The extinction of the European aurochs, or wild ox, as late as 1627 appears to have been a simple result of overenthusiastic hunting. For more than a thousand years the Dutch have been pushing back the North Sea, reclaiming the Zuider Zee. Have any species of animals, birds, or plant life vanished in the process? Have ecological values been overlooked to the extent that human life in the Netherlands has been impaired? Such questions are for the most part unasked and unanswered.

Throughout history man's treatment of nature has produced sad results. The firing of the first cannons in the early fourteenth century sent workers scrambling to the forests and valleys for more potash, iron ore, and sulfur, resulting in erosion and deforestation. A war fought with hydrogen bombs would alter the genetics of all remaining life on this planet. Our current population explosion, planless urbanization, uncontrolled dumping of sewage and garbage, and excessive industrial and private pollution have made the ecological crisis a depressing reality.

This crisis is partly a product of modern science and technology. White therefore doubts that a disastrous "ecological backlash" can be avoided simply by applying more science and more technology to our problems. He considers the solution to lie essentially in man's development of a positive value system in relation to his environment.

Jablonski (1967) considers the major problem one of ultimate freedom. Man is moving in a revolving door: Modern times demand urban living, and urban living accelerates pollution; pollutants are produced by industrialization, which is the child of increased technological development. Within this framework, not only is man's existence in danger, but his cultural fabric is also being torn apart. A high degree of interrelationship exists, so that every significant change affects many areas of life and man must continue to be most skilled in the practice of survival.

Throughout the United States, citizens are becoming increasingly concerned about pollution. Various controls, including taxation, have been proposed. Senator William Proxmire proposed a system of effluent changes under which industries would pay by the pound for pollutants discharged into the water. ("Cleaning Up the National Mess," 1970, p. 61) Related proposals have been made to place taxes on pollution of air and other natural resources. Efforts to control pollution through enforcement of codes, ordinances, and similar means are extremely important, but we must be careful to avoid indirectly penalizing the general public through such enforcement. For example, a utility forced to change from one type of fuel to another at a substantial increase in cost would very likely pass the increase on to the consuming public in higher rates. It will take hundreds of millions of dollars to restore the environment in the United States, if indeed it can be done, and in the final analysis the consumer will pay the bill.

According to David Sive, one of the nation's leading environmental lawyers, it is still unsettled whether or not we have a constitutional right to a decent environment (Pekkanen, 1970). Sive has also noted that we need many new laws to define the people's rights to land, water, and air. It may well be that restrictions on the use of land and water are our only practical methods of avoiding overexploitation of resources. Odum (1969) has urged law schools to establish departments or institutes on "landscape law" and to train "landscape lawyers" who will be capable not only of clarifying existing procedures but also of drawing up new legislation for consideration by state and national government.

A group of California legislative experts has developed "ten commandments" for promoting local environmental legislation. In abbreviated form they are to keep legislators informed, to associate the cause with reelection of legislators, to work through organizations, to refrain from insulting legislators, to keep a "high profile" on environmental issues, to pool resources with other organizations supporting candidates, to call for affirmative action, to present forcible arguments before formal hearings take place, to include legislators' activities in news media, to be militant ("Influencing Environmental Laws," 1970).

Plans were made under the direction of United Nations Secretary-General U Thant to hold the first global conference of member governments in June 1972 for the purpose of taking action on the massive environmental problems faced by mankind. "Only One Earth" was selected as the official conference slogan; Stockholm, Sweden, as the site; and the depiction of man as part master and part creature of his environment, as the emblem (which also appears on four 1972 postage stamps issued by the UN Postal Administration) ("Official Emblem for Conference on Human Environment," 1971). U Thant's initial planning report related the deterioration of the environment to three basic causes: population growth, urbanization, and the advent of new technology ("Science and Citizen," 1969). In addition, he identified four groups of substantive problems: human settlement and industrial development, use and development of natural resources, environmental pollution, and maintenance of human environmental values.

An example of progressive government action at the state level is the development and enforcement of new air-quality standards in the state of North Carolina. There are strict controls on the open burning of refuse and the emission of dark smoke into the air. The Air Pollution Control Division of the North Carolina Department of Water and Air Resources has been compiling a list of individuals and firms that do not meet the standards. Violators, including cities, schools, businesses, and industries will receive written notices. Each polluter must submit technical plans and proposed schedules for compliance. The division is authorized to take violators to court, and the polluter can be fined up to $1,000 a day until he complies.

Smoke emission from fuel-burning plants must not be darker than no. 2 on the Ringelman Chart, a U.S. Bureau of Mines publication, for more than five minutes in an hour or twenty minutes in any twenty-four-hour period. Standards for maximum levels of sulfur oxides and particulate matter in the state's air have also been established.

Reorganizing National Priorities

In order to improve the quality of the environment significantly, it is imperative that we reorganize our national priorities. In 1969 the National Wildlife Federation sponsored a Gallup poll revealing that 85 percent of the American public was concerned about the environment. A follow-up study by another independent polling organization found an overwhelming 97 percent of the American public in favor of reallocating funds from other areas of Federal spending to provide more money for environmental cleanup and protection.

On February 2, 1970, the U.S. Bureau of the Budget released a handsome little publication entitled *The Budget in Brief: Fiscal Year 1971*. The outlays of the Federal government are grouped into thirteen functional categories, and in the subbasement of fiscal priority are natural resources (see Figure 1.1 and Table 1.2).

The breakdown of expenditures on national resources is also instructive (see Figure 1.2).

Table 1.2. Expenditures on Natural Resources

Fiscal Year	Total Outlays (in Millions of Dollars)	Percentage of Total Budget Outlays
1971 (estimate)	2,503	1.2
1970 (estimate)	2,485	1.3
1969	2,129	1.2
1968	1,702	1.0
1967	1,860	1.2
1966	2,035	1.5
1965	2,063	1.7
1964	1,972	1.7
1963	1,505	1.4
1962	1,686	1.6
1961	1,568	1.6
1960	1,019	1.1

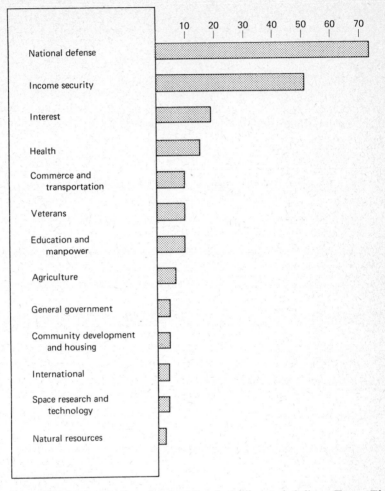

Figure 1.1 1971 budget outlays by function in billions of dollars. From *The Budget in Brief: Fiscal Year 1971.*

The environmental problem is a global one requiring global solutions. If we, as individuals and as nations, fail to help find such solutions, the consequences may be insurmountable.

REASONS FOR INSENSITIVITY
TO ENVIRONMENTAL PROBLEMS

Many of our environmental problems are primarily problems of human behavior. The insensitivity of our citizens to such problems can be docu-

Total 1971 Outlays: $2,503 Million

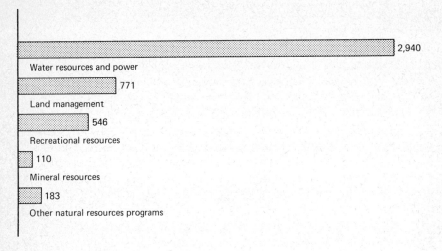

Water resources and power — 2,940

Land management — 771

Recreational resources — 546

Mineral resources — 110

Other natural resources programs — 183

Figure 1.2 1971 budget outlays for natural resources by function. From *The Budget in Brief: Fiscal Year 1971.*

mented by research. One study (Williams & Edmisten, 1965) was conducted in Nashville, Tennessee, which suffers severe air pollution, to determine how concerned citizens were. Of more than 2,000 people surveyed, only 3 percent said that measures to reduce air pollution should be enacted.

A study (Vaughn & Harlow, 1965) of the lower Detroit River concluded that it was unsuitable for water sports, other municipal recreation, fish and wildlife propagation, and navigation because it was so polluted with bacteria and chemicals. A survey of the owners and operators of boat liveries and launching ramps along the river revealed that a majority blamed inclement weather, rather than the quality of the river water, for the decline in their businesses.

Why are people so insensitive to these problems? Why do they not initiate positive action? There are too many reasons to mention here. Many people believe that technology will automatically solve the problems and that there is therefore no cause for concern. Others consider pollution a small price to pay for the prosperity associated with expanding industries, increased urbanization, and more and larger automobiles. Because environmental problems emerge slowly and result from many contributing factors, we are not always able to "see" them evolving. It is sometimes very difficult for one individual to understand how his pollutants and complacency contribute significantly to the larger environmental situation.

DEVELOPING "ENVIRONMENTAL LITERACY" IN ELEMENTARY SCHOOLS

The United States has become a predominantly urban nation. By 1980 eight out of ten Americans will probably live in metropolitan complexes. As a result of this urbanization, most Americans have very little direct contact with natural elements. Even more significant, their awareness of dependence upon such elements has correspondingly declined.

One major cause of our present crisis is thus ignorance of how to live "with" the land instead of "against" it. If we are to overcome this ignorance and develop informed, active citizens, we must begin with excellent early training. Our young should begin in their formative years to learn how to take care of the natural resources basic to their very lives and to shape the various interrelations of man, nature, and the man-made environment.

It is imperative that we help children to develop protective attitudes toward their environment and related activities very early in life. The school should be a major instrument—and model—in this development. It should take an active role in helping parents to understand their responsibility to join in training citizens who can and will contribute positively toward improving environmental quality.

The process of helping children to become aware of their environment and its problems should begin even before formal schooling and should certainly be emphasized in the elementary school. What is environmental education, and how is it different from either outdoor or conservation education? Swan's explanation is succinct:

> Environmental education may be conceived as being directed toward developing a citizenry that is knowledgeable about its environment and its associated problems, aware of the opportunities for citizen participation in environmental problem solving, and motivated to take part in such problem solving. It might be said, therefore, that environmental education is concerned with developing informed attitudes of concern for environmental quality.
>
> Environmental education is different in that it is concerned with involving people in environmental problem solving. It makes no claims to making people naturalists. Undoubtedly many students exposed to an environmental education program would become interested in nature, but this is a secondary benefit rather than a primary aim. (Swan, 1969, p. 28)

Most programs in conservation education are oriented toward basic natural resources, often neglecting overwhelming problems of the man-made environment. In addition to understanding that his welfare depends upon proper management and use of natural resources, man should be aware of community problems: improper use of pesticides, lack of environmental planning, community pollution in many forms, and absence of programs and services to cope effectively with environmental problems.

Environmental-education programs in elementary schools should be interdisciplinary, incorporating material from ecology, biology, chemistry, physics, and earth science. Understanding of the social aspects of the environment may be developed through study of the findings of psychology, sociology, history, political science, economics, and other social sciences. It is important for children to understand ecological concepts, principles, and processes. It is equally important for them to develop restraint, concern, and a value system that encourages positive action to improve the environment.

A few communities in the nation have recognized the challenge of environmental education and are trying to provide it in their elementary schools. Usually, however, such education is either incidental or altogether absent from elementary-school curricula. There is an urgent need for a dynamic type of environmental education curriculum in our schools, one that will be in tune with emerging problems and trends both today and tomorrow.

First of all, public support for such education must be generated. State and local environmental-education committees should be formed to formulate policies on curriculum, standards of instruction, teacher preparation, and so on; to spread understanding of environmental problems and issues; and to coordinate resources for developing environmental-education programs; and to raise funds and see that expenditures are made wisely.

State departments of education, in cooperation with local school divisions, must provide leadership in developing environmental-education curricula, materials, workshops for preservice and in-service teachers, and related activities.

Environmental studies for young children should be based upon a stimulating teaching philosophy. Klimes (1970) has identified several guidelines for involving the young in the study of their environment. First, he reminds us that we need to inform our teaching with a sense of wonder, of discovery. Second, young people have to be helped to understand that there is nothing mysterious about the ecological point of view. They must focus on the source of environmental problems and recognize that common sense is necessary in finding solutions. Third, we must help young people to become aware of and to appreciate the great diversity of our environment. We must help students to understand that it took millions of years for delicate ecological interrelations to develop and that man has created havoc by disrupting them. Students should also understand that nature has its own systems of checks and balances; we must take them outside the four walls of the classroom to see these processes in action if we are to stimulate discussion and action.

Former U.S. Commissioner of Education James E. Allen, Jr., has emphasized environmental education as the key to human survival:

> Why do I say that education is the key to survival? Why not new laws? Why not new rules and regulations and codes and all the rest of the complex apparatus of government which regulates nearly all human endeavor? Why is education more important than all of these admittedly important measures?
>
> The answer is that in a free society it is always the citizen who must bear the ultimate responsibility for the choices that are made and the actions that are taken. In all our history we have found no better way than through the process of education for equipping citizens— you and me and our children—with the knowledge and understanding needed to make these choices and to take these actions. (Allen, 1970, p. 23)

Three specific tasks of environmental education are generating *awareness* of how man and his technology affect and are affected by the environment, *concern* for reestablishing and re-creating balanced relations among all forms of life, and *motivation and training* to solve current problems and prevent future ones.

The major objective is to train citizens who understand clearly that man is an inseparable part of the world system and that his continued existence is thus totally dependent upon the continued functioning of that system.

SUMMARY

If we as professional educators are effectively to engage pupils in a study of the environment, it is most important that we ourselves learn more about environmental problems and issues and related ecological concepts and processes.

Environmental-education programs in elementary schools should incorporate concepts and processes from both the natural and social sciences. The emphasis should be upon helping children to understand man's interrelations with both the natural and man-made components of their environment. The ultimate objective is to produce informed and active citizens.

The development of an effective environmental-education curriculum for elementary schools poses a tremendous challenge, but it is a key to human survival. Environmental education can become a reality only if we care and act.

INVESTIGATIONS

1. How ecologically aware are the citizens in your community? What is the level of ecological awareness among the students and teachers in your school? Construct an ecological-awareness inventory and conduct a random-sample survey of citizens, students, and teachers. Analyze your findings. What are their implications?

2. List what you suspect are the major environmental problems in your community. Conduct a random sample of citizen opinions about environmental problems in the community and compare results. Collect data relative to the level of air, water, and sound pollution in your community. Compare with data from similar types of communities.

3. Brandwein has proposed an "environmental bill of rights." What are the implications of his suggestions for man in the latter part of this century?

4. Investigate current and proposed national, state, and local legislation related to the environment. Invite an expert to discuss such legislation in class.

5. What are the major industries in your community doing to improve the quality of the environment? Conduct a study, and report your findings for class discussion.

6. Outline the major points of your philosophy for engaging children in a study of the environment. Compare your ideas with those of others. Then read Klimes (1970). Does he alter your thinking?

7. Read Darling and Milton (1966). Then write an essay entitled "Environment in the United States, 1999."

8. Marine (1969) has outlined his thesis of the "engineering mentality." What data can you collect on whether or not this concept is at work in your community? Can you cite specific examples?

9. Visit a random sample of elementary schools in your community, and find out whether or not they have environmental-education programs. If so, identify the characteristics of such programs.

10. Study your state and local budgets for the current fiscal year. What emphasis is given to environmental matters? What can be done to raise the priority of such expenditures?

11. Why is man so insensitive to his environment? Cite examples in your community. What can you do to develop your own environmental

sensitivity? How can you help others to develop environmental awareness?

REFERENCES

Allen, James E., Jr. "Education for Survival," *American Education*, 6:19–23, March 1970.

Association for Supervision and Curriculum Development. *A.S.C.D. Resolutions, 1970–71.* Washington, D.C.: National Education Association, January 1970.

Brandwein, Paul F. "Needed: An Environmental Bill of Rights," *American Forests*, 76:28–31, April 1970.

Carson, Rachel. *Silent Spring.* Boston: Houghton-Mifflin, 1962.

"Cleaning Up the National Mess: How Great the Cost? Who Will Pay?" *Time,* 95:60–61, February 2, 1970.

Darling, F. Fraser & John P. Milton (eds.). *Future Environments of North America.* Garden City, N.Y.: Natural History Press, 1966.

Ehrlich, Paul R. "Paying the Piper," *New Scientist*, 36:652–655, March 1967.

Everett, Glenn D. "One Man's Family," in Garret Harden, ed., *Population, Evolution, and Birth Control.* San Francisco: Freeman, 1967, pp. 41–44.

Gates, David M. *This Week in Public Health*, Massachusetts Department of Public Health, 17:332–334, No. 34, August 19, 1968.

"Influencing Environmental Laws," *Saturday Review*, 53:58, April 4, 1970.

Ingraham, Holliss. "Pure Waters, the Silent Crisis." Address delivered at the Mohawk-Hudson River Conference on Water Pollution, Albany, December 12, 1967.

Jablonski, John R. "Man, Culture, Evolution and Environment," *Christian Century*, 84:495–498, April 19, 1967.

Klimes, John. "Education and Our Ecological Crisis," *Science and Children,* 7:30–31, March 1970.

Marine, Gene. *America the Raped.* New York: Simon & Schuster, 1969.

Odum, Eugene P. "The Strategy of Ecosystem Development," *Science*, 164:269, April 18, 1969.

"Official Emblem for Conference on Human Environment," *School and Society*, 99:332–333, October 1971.

Paddock, William & Paul Paddock. *Famine—1975! America's Decision: Who Will Survive?* Boston: Little, Brown, 1967.

Pekkanen, John. "Ecology: A Cause Becomes a Mass Movement," *Life,* 68:22–30, January 30, 1970.

President's Science Advisory Committee, Environmental Pollution Panel. *Restoring the Quality of Our Environment.* Washington, D.C.: White House, 1965.

"Science and Citizen," *Scientific American*, 221:48, August 1969.

Swan, James. "The Challenge of Environmental Education," *Phi Delta Kappan,* 51:27–28, September 1969.

U.S. Bureau of the Budget. *Budget in Brief: Fiscal Year 1971.* Washington, D.C.: Government Printing Office, 1970.

Vaughn, R. D. & G. L. Harlow. *Findings: Conference in the Matter of the Pollution of the Detroit River, Michigan Waters of Lake Erie and their Tributaries in the State of Michigan.* Washington, D.C.: U.S. Public Health Service, 1965.

White, Lynn, Jr. "The Historical Roots of Our Ecologic Crisis," *Science,* 155:1202–1207, March 10, 1967.

Williams, James & Norman Edmisten. *An Air Resources Management Plan for the Nashville Metropolitan Area.* Cincinnati: U.S. Public Health Service Division of Air Pollution Control, 1965.

chapter 2 / what the elementary-school teacher must know about ecology

Anyone who has gone fishing, eaten a picnic in the woods, or watched tadpoles grow into frogs has learned a little bit about ecology. Ecology involves the study of natural laws that control living things. Every living thing is affected not only by its neighbors but also by its inorganic surroundings. This whole system is called an "ecosystem." It can be of any size: a quart jar, a pond, or an ocean, for example. In this chapter we shall explore some of the major concepts and principles of ecology that we must employ as we involve children in environmental education.

Man must live with the environment, using its resources judiciously, or face extermination. The interrelations of organisms and their environment are most important; ecology, which is the study of these interrelations, therefore also becomes increasingly important each day. In fact, never in the history of mankind has there been a greater need for understanding and application of ecological principles than there is today.

AN APPROACH TO THE STUDY OF ECOLOGY

Clarke (1954) believes that the study of ecology is best begun with analysis of individual environmental influences and identification of the various activities of organisms, as steps toward understanding the dynamic interaction between the total environment and its inhabitants. Fundamental relations are most easily grasped through analysis of simple situations before progressing to more complex ones. It must be emphasized that any phase of ecology is focused on a reciprocal relationship between an organism and its environment. Knight has illustrated this point:

If we consider a pine tree in its natural forest setting we find that the pine is subject to environmental influences such as soil, water, wind, soil minerals, the amount of soil, oxygen, atmospheric carbon dioxide, the amount of sunlight, the prevailing temperatures and countless other abiotic or non-living factors. In addition there are the biotic or living elements of the environments such as bark beetles, birds, squirrels, soil bacteria and fungi, worms, and parasites of various types, all of which may directly or indirectly affect the tree. The tree in turn will modify the surrounding environment: the shade produced will alter temperatures; its limbs will prevent the free flow of air; transpiration, or water loss from leaf surfaces will alter the humidity of the air; its roots will penetrate the soil, opening up soil channels, and root hairs will extract water from soil spaces, so that the entire soil environment will be modified. (Knight, 1965, p. 2)

This kind of reciprocal activity is also characteristic of man, who must learn to function in harmony with the environmental system and not apart from it.

The initial human use of ecological data may be traced back to prehistoric man, who relied on clues from his environment to find food and shelter, in order to survive. Ecology emerged as a formal science in the mid-1800s. Reiter appears to have been the first to combine the Greek roots *oikos* ("house") and *logos* ("study [of]") to obtain the term "ecology" in 1865 (Knight, p. 8). In 1866 Haeckle defined ecology as the body of knowledge relating to the economy of nature, the investigation of the total relations of animals to their organic and inorganic environment. Although the majority of formal definitions of ecology approximate that of Haeckle but include plants as well, a few seem sharply different. For example, Elton has defined ecology as "scientific natural history," the sociology and economics of animals (1949, p. 5). Shelford has defined it as a "science of the community" (1963, p. 15), and Odum has emphasized the study of the "structure and function of nature" (1959, p. 4). Whether or not any one of these definitions precisely delineates the area of inquiry proper to ecology is debatable. Ecology is a broad-based science, and its parameters become progressively difficult to identify as the environment itself becomes more complex.

During the first third of this century the total volume of written materials on ecology surpassed that produced during all previous history. As a result of increased interest and research in ecology a number of other, related disciplines have emerged, including:

1. *Paleoecology*, the study of environmental conditions and life as it existed in past ages.

2. *Zoogeography*, the scientific study of the geographic distribution of animals.
3. *Limnology*, the study of the living and nonliving components of inland waters.
4. *Oceanography*, the study of the biotic and physical conditions in oceans, bays, and estuaries.
5. *Ethology*, the study of relations between animals and their environments.

As we become more familiar with ecological studies, we recognize two major kinds of investigators: the *autecologist*, who is interested in a single species or a few closely related species and how they interact with the environment, and the *synecologist*, who deals with the structure, development, and distribution of ecological communities.

MAJOR ECOLOGICAL CONCEPTS

Every discipline has its own basic elements, terminology, and principles. Saylor and Alexander (1966) have defined a discipline as an organized body of knowledge about a unique domain, for which basic rules or definitions are formulated to determine what falls inside and outside the domain, with a recognized structure for organizing new knowledge. Ford and Pugno (1964) have described the structure of a discipline as a set of fundamental generalizations, principles, rules, propositions, or basic abstractions that unite a body of knowledge into a coherent whole. Bruner has demonstrated the application of such definitions to biology:

> Take first a set of observations on an inchworm crossing a sheet of graph paper mounted on a board. The board is horizontal; the animal moves in a straight line. We tilt the board so that the inclined plane or upward grade is 30 degrees. We observe that the animal does not go straight up but travels at an angle of 45 degrees from the line of maximum climb. We now tilt the board to 60 degrees. At what angle does the animal travel with respect to the line of maximum climb? Now, say he travels along a line 75 degrees off the straight-up line. (From these two measures we may infer that inchworms prefer to travel uphill, if uphill they must go, along an incline of 15 degrees.) We have discovered a tropism, as it is called, indeed a geotropism. It is not an isolated fact. We can go on to show that among simple organisms, such phenomena—regulation of locomotion according to a fixed or built-in standard—are the rule. There is a preferred level of illumination toward which lower organisms orient, a preferred level of salinity, of temperature, and so on. Once a student grasps this basic relation between external stimulation and locomotor action, he is well on his way toward

being able to handle a good deal of seemingly new but, in fact, highly related information. (Bruner, 1960, pp. 6–7)

Although it is not imperative for the elementary-school teacher to be a specialist in ecology in order to engage pupils in environmental learning effectively, it is most important that he understand the basic structure of ecology. Such understandings should enable him to plan intellectually honest instructional experiences.

Limiting Factors

All plants and animals have ranges of tolerance for certain environmental factors. More specifically, an organism may survive, provided that environmental elements are maintained within critical limits. One sea organism may be able to tolerate a relatively low temperature and high salt content, whereas another can tolerate the high salt content but requires a much higher temperature for survival. When a critical environmental factor falls above or below the tolerable range for a given species, it becomes a limiting factor. In 1963 Shelford stated his law of tolerance: that a value below a critical minimum or above a critical maximum will exclude certain organisms from environmental areas. Since Shelford's law was formulated, considerable research has revealed that a plant or animal may have quite a wide range of tolerance for another factor in its environment. Within a particular geographical region, over hundreds of years of adaptation, genetic change, and selection, locally adapted populations, called "ecotypes," may develop. "Ecotype" was defined by Turesson (1922) as the product of the genotypical response of an ecospecies to a particular habitat.

Ecosystem

According to Evans (1956) the term "ecosystem" was first proposed by Tansley in 1935. Basically it refers to the circulation, transformation, and accumulation of energy and matter through the medium of living things. Photosynthesis, decomposition, predation, and parasitism are among the principal biological processes responsible for the movement and storage of materials. Circulation of energy and matter in the inorganic part of the ecosystem is also facilitated by such processes as evaporation, precipitation, and erosion. Additional characteristics of an ecosystem include regulatory mechanisms like processes of growth and reproduction, patterns of immigration, and adaptive habits.

The fundamental steps in the operation of the ecosystem have been stated by Clarke: "(1) reception of energy; (2) production of organic material by producers; (3) consumption of this material by consumers and its further elaboration; (4) decomposition to inorganic compounds; and

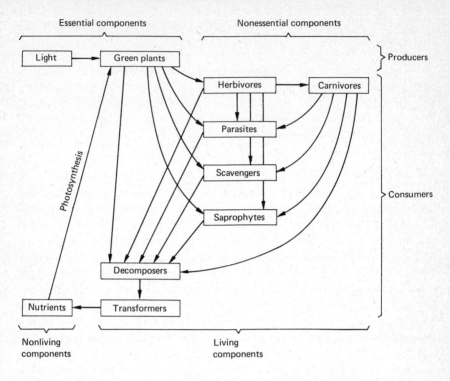

Figure 2.1 Principal steps and components in a self-sufficient ecosystem. From George L. Clarke, *Elements of Ecology,* rev. ed. (New York: John Wiley & Sons, Inc., 1965).

(5) transformation to forms suitable for the nutrition of the producers" (1954, pp. 466–467; see Figure 2.1). An ecosystem is thus, very simply, a basic ecological unit comprising living and nonliving components inter-acting to produce a stable system.

In the past man has taken for granted the gas-exchange, water-purification, nutrient-cycling, and other protective functions of self-sufficient ecosystems, primarily because neither his numbers nor his environmental manipulations have been so great as to affect regional and global balances seriously. This situation is now changing, and a form of ecosystem analysis in which man is considered as part of the environment must be applied.

Odum (1959) has defined ecology as the study of the structure and functions of ecosystems. By "structure" he means the composition of the biological community, including species, numbers, life history and spatial distribution of populations, quantity and characteristics of nonbiotic materials, and the range of conditions like temperature and light. By "functions" he means the rates of production and respiration of the populations, the rates of material or nutrient cycling, and the regulation of environment by organisms.

The basic energy cycle may serve to illustrate the concept of an ecosystem. Green plants derive energy from the sun. Herbivorous and carnivorous animals obtain energy from other plants and animals. Bacteria and fungi draw energy from the decomposition of dead organisms. Within the ecosystem there is therefore a continuous flow of energy, with some retained and some lost to the atmosphere at each stage.

In a broad sense there are two major types of ecosystems, terrestrial and aquatic. Each has subdivisions, for example, fresh-water and marine aquatic ecosystems. Among terrestrial ecosystems are prairies, forests, and tundra; these major subdivisions are called "biomes" (see Figure 2.2).

Aquatic ecosystems occupy more than 70 percent of the total area of the globe. As they are much more uniform in conditions favorable or unfavorable to life than are land areas, they are not as fully subclassified as are terrestrial ecosystems. Classifications are frequently based on major climatic differences, size and relative permanence of the body of water, and water depth. Life in the oceans, as in fresh waters, is very dependent upon the chemical properties of the water.

Biological Community

The term "community biota," or simply "community" generally refers to all plants and animals that occupy a specific area. The focus is on the interdependence of plants and animals, an interacting population of various species. Species that exercise control over the community are called "dominant." Natural terrestrial communities are most often dominated by plants, which reduce the density of light, hold down soil moisture, and crowd or display general intolerance for other species. Animals, particularly when they are present in large numbers and have destructive feeding habits, are also sometimes dominant.

Population density and distribution within a community are dependent upon many factors. Certain species of plants and animals are very dependent upon soil and water and relatively independent of climate. Most plants and animals are very dependent upon all three. The density of a population is measured by the number of individuals in a specific area of the habitat over a particular period of time. The maximum possible density is known as the saturation point. Overpopulation usually tends ultimately to decrease density. Weaker members of the population die in the keen competition for food and shelter. Predation usually increases. Diseases and

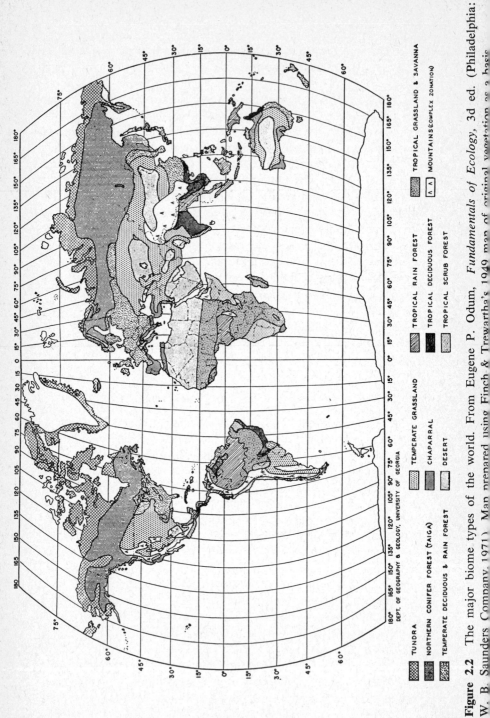

Figure 2.2 The major biome types of the world. From Eugene P. Odum, *Fundamentals of Ecology*, 3d ed. (Philadelphia: W. B. Saunders Company, 1971). Map prepared using Finch & Trewartha's 1949 map of original vegetation as a basis.

parasitism also often increase in overpopulated areas. Underpopulation may encourage increases in density as a result of a greater abundance of food, shelter, and water. But when populations are reduced beyond a certain point they may become extinct.

Knight (1965) has described several classifications of communities. First, they may be divided between two major categories. "Abstract" communities consist of broadly defined groupings according to certain types of features. A "concrete" community is composed of plants and animals from a specific area. The total of life, all the plants and animals of the world, compose the global community. It can be subdivided into continental and oceanic communities. A biotic province is a geographical area with uniform climatic or physiographic features, the Carolinian or Montanan community, for example. All these examples are abstract communities (see Figure 2.3).

A "stand" is a small, concrete portion of a larger community: a

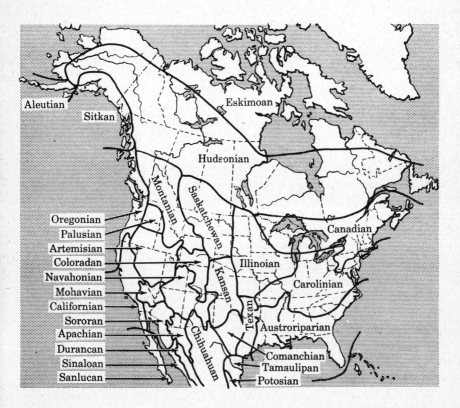

Figure 2.3 The biotic provinces of North America according to Lee R. Dice. Reprinted with permission of the Macmillan Company from *Basic Concepts of Ecology* by Clifford B. Knight. Copyright © by Clifford B. Knight, 1965.

particular forest, lake, swamp, or river. Each individual plant or animal in a stand is a microstand.

In addition to permanent and semipermanent communities, there are mobile communities like insect colonies and flocks of birds. Although ecologists are not in complete agreement on all the details of these classifications, the general framework is useful.

Life Cycles

The life spans and reproductive cycles of individual plants and animals are most interesting. Dominant plants like trees may live 30–100 times as long as do such forest mammals as deer. The length of time from birth to reproductive maturity is approximately one and a half years for deer and twelve to twenty years for certain trees.

Knight (1965) has emphasized the controlling influence of the activity sequence during the seasonal and twenty-four-hour cycles. In man changes in body temperature, blood pressure, kidney functioning and related processes are adjusted to a standard twenty-four-hour cycle. Research has indicated that men who have been forced to live on briefer or irregular time schedules have become less efficient and have performed under greater physiological stress. Biologists have demonstrated the presence of such cyclical rhythms in various plants as well. Wilhelm Pfeffer, the German plant physiologist, has demonstrated it in the bean seedling (Knight, p. 245). In his experiment, the first pair of leaves above the cotyledons were elevated during the day and dropped some distance at night. This was not a response brought about by variations in temperature or illumination because the bean seedling functioned in the same manner when both of these factors remained unchanged. Later, other researchers discovered that this rhythm occurs during the twenty-four-hour period regardless of the stimuli. It appears that daily and seasonal periodicity (natural response) is almost universal among plants and animals.

Biological activity requires the use of energy, all of which comes ultimately from the sun. Solar energy is transformed from radiant to chemical form through photosynthesis and from chemical to mechanical forms through cellular metabolism. Only about one fifty-millionth of the sun's energy output reaches the earth's outer atmosphere. This energy flows at a constant rate and is called the "solar flux." Half or more of the solar flux is lost as it passes through the earth's atmosphere: dispersed by clouds and dust particles or absorbed by ozone, oxygen, and water vapor. Ecologists are particularly interested in energy flows within ecosystems. Figure 2.4 illustrates the various inputs and uses of energy within a schematic ecosystem.

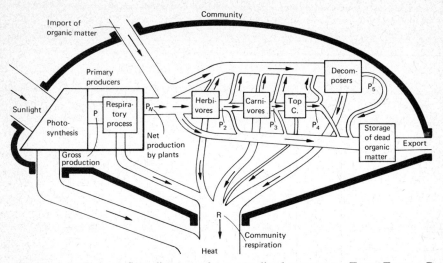

Figure 2.4 Energy flow diagram of a generalized ecosystem. From Eugene P. Odum, *Fundamentals of Ecology,* 3d ed. (Philadelphia: W. B. Saunders Company, 1971).

We must understand the various movement patterns of nutrients in the production of energy. There are three basic types. The first is the *hydrologic cycle,* involving a never-ending circulation of water between the surface of the earth and the atmosphere through precipitation and evaporation (see Figure 2.5). The amount of precipitation in a given area is determined primarily by atmospheric circulation and topography. The rate and amount of evaporation are as critical as are the rate and amount of precipitation in determining the distribution of particular types of ecosystems.

The *gaseous nutrient* cycles involve such elements as carbon and nitrogen. The natural carbon cycle (Figure 2.6) returns carbon to the environment at about the same rate as that at which it is removed. For this reason Kormondy (1969) has argued that the carbon cycle is an almost perfect cycle. Recent research has, however, predicted a substantial increase in atmospheric carbon dioxide (CO_2) by the end of this century. The nitrogen cycle is very similar to that of carbon.

In the *sedimentary cycle,* the lithosphere serves as a major reservoir for such elements as phosphorous, sulfur, and iodine. Sulfur enters the atmosphere in sulfur dioxide, which results from incomplete combustion of fossil fuels. Sulfur dioxide is a major source of air pollution today. Large concentrations of hydrogen sulfide, another sulfur compound, are often responsible for the death of aquatic animals, particularly fish. The sedimentation characteristics of sulfur may have great influence upon ecosystems. Significant sulfur sedimentation, or stagnation, may be found in the ocean and in deep-water lakes like Lake Superior.

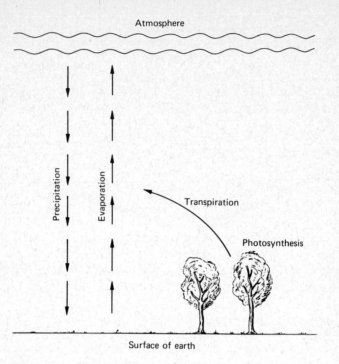

Figure 2.5 The hydrologic cycle.

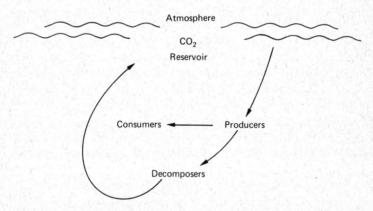

Figure 2.6 The carbon cycle.

There are three major kinds of nutritional process:

1. *Autotrophic*, or self-nourishing, organisms can synthesize all essential organic components entirely from inorganic substances and are not directly dependent upon other organisms for food. This group consists primarily of green plants.

2. *Heterotrophic* organisms require already formed organic compounds and are thus dependent upon autotrophic organisms. This group includes the various bacteria, fungi, and parasites.
3. *Mixotrophic* organisms are capable of both autotrophic and heterotrophic nutrition. For example, insect-eating plants also participate in photosynthesis.

Ecologists are concerned not only about the types of nutrients in an ecosystem but also about the input and output rates of such nutrients. Man should understand in particular how his activities influence the various energy cycles within his environment.

The Importance of Habitat

Elton (1949) has defined "habitat" as an area of uniform physiography, vegetation, climate, and any other trait that the investigator believes important. It is a place where a plant or animal naturally lives. Habitats vary in size, from a forest or oceanic area measured in acres or square miles to the surface of a leaf measured in centimeters or millimeters.

Each habitat possesses unique environmental conditions, though similar conditions may prevail in habitats of the same type in distant places. For example, temperature, wind movement, and humidity may vary considerably even between the treetops of a forest and the forest floor or the root-soil area below. Primary habitats include bare areas of volcanic rock and ash, river silt and sand, and sand deposited by wind. They are often modified and enriched by such fertilizing agents as burrowing animals, animal droppings, plant seeds, roots, and decomposing organic matter. The habitat may be influenced by abiotic, or nonliving, factors like wind, carbon dioxide, sunlight, temperature, and earthquakes, and by such biotic factors as soil bacteria and fungi, worms, parasites, men, and various other animals.

Improvement of the habitat is a continuous ecological concern; in recent years it has emerged as one of the foci of wildlife management. For example, placing log dams at intervals along shaded streams provides pools for trout, which require a constant flow of cool water. There are thousands of other ways in which ecologists are assisting in habitat development and improvement.

Dasmann (1968) has emphasized that the most promising approach to conservation takes into account the ecology of man. The major objectives of conservation should be to develop an area in order to provide the greatest improvement in quality of life for mankind.

THE ECOLOGY OF POPULATIONS

Ecologists are interested in many aspects of population but primarily in growth, regulation, and interaction. These major categories can be subdivided into birth and death rates; forms of growth; fluctuation, oscillation, and dispersion; and cooperation and competition.

In 1798 Thomas Malthus wrote one of the most significant works on population ever published. He gloomily predicted that population would increase faster than the productive power associated with more people. Malthus indicated that the population could double every generation if each woman had only four surviving children, half of them girls, who would produce more children in the next generation. He thought that this might produce a geometrical population increase—2, 4, 8, 16, 32, 64, and so on—with a doubling each generation. He argued that the world's land could not increase its food output at this rate. Thus, if population was not checked by moral restraint, it would have to be checked by famine as the population outran the food supply (Bach, 1968, p. 201).

The reproductive potential of a population is influenced by natality; mortality; morbidity; competition for food, shelter, and mates; predation; and parasitisms. Natality is the greatest number of organisms that can be produced by one species in a specific unit of time. An organism seldom reaches its maximum potential because of various environmental factors. The *normal*, or *observed*, *natality rate* is one that can actually be measured over a specific period of time. It is computed by dividing the number of births by the time unit.

Mortality usually results from the coincidence of multiple factors. Some of the major contributing factors include the following: hereditary diseases, other diseases, and parasitism. The mortality rate is computed by dividing the number of deaths by a specific unit of time. Mortality rates are, however, more difficult to determine than are birth rates, at least for certain kinds of population. Scavengers, bacteria, and predation make it extremely difficult to identify dead organisms. Population stability requires a definite relationship between natality and mortality. The *density* of a population is critical, for competition for vital necessities and parasitism are often commonplace in overpopulated areas. *Morbidity*, the relative incidence of disease, also influences density.

As a result of all these and related factors, total population size is constantly in flux. The combination of factors that limit it is called *environmental resistance*. The maximum possible rate of increase for a population occurs when the natality rate is the highest possible for the species and the mortality rate is the lowest.

Predation and *parasitism* are different yet related. A parasite is essentially an organism that resides on or in the body of a larger living organism and nourishes upon the host's tissues. The typical predator is more mobile but devours individuals of specific other species. There are exceptions, but these definitions serve as working concepts. In general, parasites benefit at the expense of the strong, whereas predators exploit the weak. Borderline instances include barnacles growing on the back of a whale, for

they do not feed on the host's tissues, blood-sucking insects are also difficult to categorize. Plant fungi, bacteria, mosquito larvae, and various forms
of protozoa are clear-cut examples of parasites. Some parasites even feed
on other parasites; for example, fleas can be hosts to smaller fleas.

Some parasites are known to require multiple hosts for the completion of their life cycles. Clarke has provided an example:

> The bass tapeworm that causes stunting and sterility in the small-
> mouthed bass also illustrates the complexities of multiple parasitism. In
> the spring when the bass swims into the shoal water of a lake for
> spawning, segments of the tapeworm living in the fish's gut are dis-
> charged into the water where they produce eggs. The eggs are eaten by
> copepods, a secondary host, and hatch out within the alimentary tract
> of these primitive crustaceans. The resulting larvae pass through the
> wall of the intestines into the body cavity of this host. Meanwhile young
> bass and other fish spawned in the same shore area have grown to the
> feeding stage and eat the copepods harboring the larvae of the tape-
> worm. A close correlation is thus required between the time for the
> copepod population to develop, for the larvae of the parasite to hatch,
> and for the young fish to appear. The larvae taken in with the copepods
> can resist being digested, as can the other stages of the parasite, and
> make their way into the body cavity, liver, or other organs of the small
> fish which is a tertiary host. When the infected young fishes are eaten
> by the voracious larger bass, the tapeworm larvae are passed on, and
> this transfer from smaller fish to larger fish may take place several times.
> The larvae do not develop into adults while in the body cavity or
> internal glands of the small fish. Only if the infected fish is eaten by a
> large bass at the moment when the larvae are ready to metamorphose,
> do they develop into adult tapeworms. This final stage establishes itself
> in the intestine of the primary host and thus completes the life cycle.
> (Clarke, 1954, pp. 390, 392)

Predators may be classified as *carnivores* (animal-eating) and *herbivores* (plant-eating). Most often animals eat animals or plants, but there
are plants that consume animals. A good example is the sundew (*Drosera*),
which secretes a sticky secretion that traps insects. Generally predators eat
the individual organisms that are most available or accessible.

Organisms compete for space, light, food, and other basic necessities,
but the nature of the competition varies among species. Clarke (1954) has
identified four possible results of competition between two antagonistic
species in the same environment. First, if the species have similar characteristics one may inhibit the growth of the other more than its own growth
is inhibited and thus eventually eliminate the second from the area. Second,
if the two species vary their environmental demands, they may continue
to coexist in the area. Third, if there is dependence between the two species, as between parasite and host or predator and prey, the more aggressive

may eliminate the other and turn to other food sources. Finally, if the aggressor is unable to destroy all members of the other species, the two species may continue to coexist in the area.

Perception of natural environments is very complex, involving much more than the apprehension of physical stimuli. Sight probably influences human responses to environments more immediately than do the other senses. In some instances odors—like the aroma of pine needles or the scent of a skunk—may leave more lasting impressions than does what we see. In writing of recreation-resource management Shafer (1969) has concluded that recreation consists of people's *reactions* to the outdoors. One individual may consider a tree a thing of beauty; another may see it only as a thing in the way.

TAXONOMY

Taxonomy is basic to the study of the natural environment. The broad field of study encompassing all aspects of organic diversity is called "systematics." It has two major functions: first, discovery, description, and classification of unknown species and the clarification of their relations, that is, taxonomy, and, second, identification of known organisms for private purposes or as a service to other scientists or the public.

A functional taxonomic system must be universally accepted, understood, and used. Before the middle of the eighteenth century plants and animals were known by local (vernacular) names, which varied from place to place. Latin was the scientific language used, and as new species were rapidly discovered the proliferation of Latin nomenclature became unwieldy. In 1753 Carolus Linnaeus, a Swedish botanist, presented his binomial nomenclature system. He proposed to give each species of plant and animal a name consisting of two Latin words: the name of its genus and that of its species. Each new name, accompanied by a description of the organism, was to be published in a widely circulated scientific journal, so that it would become the universally accepted name for that species. For example, the common honeybee was variously known as *apis pubescens, thorace subgriseo, abdomine fusco, pedibus posticis glabris,* and *utringue margine ciliatis*; the Linnaean name is *apis mellifica*.

Linnaeus also made a most significant contribution to hierarchical classification of plant and animal groups. Families were grouped into orders, orders into classes, and classes into phyla. The full classification of the American robin follows:

Kingdom: Animal
Phylum: *Chordata*
Class: *Aves*

Order: *Passeriformes*
Family: *Turdidae*
Genus: *Turdus*
Species: *Migratorius*
Linnaean name: *Turdus migratorius*

It is most important to know how taxonomists classify a given species; three major factors—morphological, genetic, and territorial—are taken into account. Morphological traits can be observed or measured. Genetic traits are hereditary and may reflect crossbreeding. Territorial traits include the common geographical and ecological range of the species. Benton and Werner (1966) have emphasized that morphological differences are the most useful of these criteria for classification. But new approaches are continually emerging in taxonomy. One relatively recent one is *chemotaxonomy*, based on chemical analysis of plant and animal parts. (For a more detailed treatment of this approach, see Alston and Turner, 1963.)

SOME UNIFYING PRINCIPLES OF ECOLOGY

There are many unifying principles of ecology with which teachers should become acquainted. All school children at all age levels can be introduced to these principles in appropriate ways, as we shall demonstrate in later chapters. Sixteen of these principles are summarized here.

1. All living organisms, plants or animals, have ranges of tolerance for certain environmental factors.
2. The interactions of most organisms and their environments are reciprocal.
3. An ecosystem comprises the circulation, transformation, and accumulation of energy and matter through the medium of living things and their activities.
4. A biotic community includes all plants and animals that occupy a given area. Population densities and distribution within such a community depend upon many factors.
5. The life spans and reproductive cycles of individual plants and animals depend upon energy; the sun is the primary source of energy.
6. Habitats vary in size and quality, each with its own unique conditions.
7. Organisms compete for space, light, food, and other basic necessities, but the nature of this competition varies among species.
8. The geographical range of any species is controlled by forces

within the environment; all animals and plants tend to grow, reproduce, and spread until checked by influences in the environment.

9. The community maintains itself as a working unit with all necessary exchanges in dynamic balance.

10. Modern ecology is concerned with the functional interdependencies between living things and their surroundings.

11. The world is divided into two major kinds of environments: terrestrial and aquatic.

12. Water has higher specific heat, latent heat of fusion, and latent heat of evaporation than does any other common substance.

13. Temperature is a universal influence and frequently a limiting factor in the growth and distribution of animals and plants.

14. All living things depend upon the environment for nutrition.

15. No individual animal can survive entirely by itself because it depends upon other organisms for food and other necessities.

16. Ecosystems have structure, in that different parts are arranged in definite patterns.

SUMMARY

Despite new interest in ecology, the science itself has existed for more than a century. At present it has five major branches: paleoecology, zoogeography, limnology, oceanography, and ethology. In this chapter we have introduced selected concepts related to the structure of the discipline.

INVESTIGATIONS

1. Bruner (1960) has emphasized the importance of the structure of a discipline: its unique facts, concepts, processes, and generalizations. What are the major structural elements of ecology? Contrast the structure of ecology with the structure of mathematics.

2. What are the major components and characteristics of an ecosystem? Compare an equatic ecosystem with a terrestrial ecosystem. What differences and similarities do you discover?

3. Choose an animal species that is often found near your home. Investigate the natality, mortality, morbidity, predation, and so on of its population. What is the environmental-resistance level for this animal? Why?

4. Investigate William Pfeffer's research on the twenty-four-hour cycle. What research on this cycle in man is available? You may want to

conduct your own research project. See George L. Clarke, *Elements of Ecology* (New York: Wiley, 1954), p. 217.

5. Life is dependent upon energy. The ultimate source of energy is the sun. Investigate the characteristics of solar energy, with specific attention to the processes of transforming it into forms usable by plants and animals.

6. Review several basic texts on ecology, including Knight (1965) and Kormondy (1969). Prepare an annotated handbook of key ecological concepts and terms that you believe would be helpful to a classroom teacher.

7. Identify the major ecological imbalances in your community. What appear to be the major causes of these imbalances? What can people do to ameliorate them.

8. Identify and describe specific examples of interdependence between plants and animals in your community.

9. Investigate the current status of the American bald eagle. What factors are encouraging its extinction? Can it be saved? How? Why?

10. Read Alston and Turner (1963), and examine implications for plant and animal classification.

11. Assume that you are expected to lead in developing an environmental policy for development of the moon. What ecological concepts and guidelines would you emphasize? What specific guidelines for interrelations between earth and moon can you suggest?

REFERENCES

Alston, Ralph E. & B. L. Turner. *Biochemical Systematics*. Englewood Cliffs, N.J.: Prentice-Hall, 1963.

Bach, George Leland. *Economics—An Introduction to Analysis and Policy*, 6th ed. Englewood Cliffs, N.J.: Prentice-Hall, 1968.

Benton, Allen H. & William E. Werner, Jr. *Field Biology and Ecology*. New York: McGraw-Hill, 1966.

Bruner, Jerome. *The Process of Education*. New York: Random House, 1960.

Clarke, George L. *Elements of Ecology*. New York: Wiley, 1954.

Dasmann, Raymond F. *Environmental Conservation*. New York: Wiley, 1968.

Elton, Charles. "Population Interspersion: An Essay on Animal Community Patterns," *Journal of Ecology*, 37:1–12, June 1949.

Evans, Francis C. "Ecosystem as the Basic Unit in Ecology," *Science*, 123:1127–1128, June 22, 1956.

Ford, G. W. & Lawrence Pugno (eds.). *The Structure of Knowledge and the Curriculum*. Chicago: Rand McNally, 1964.

Knight, Clifford B. *Basic Concepts of Ecology*. New York: Macmillan, 1965.

Kormondy, Edward J. *Concepts of Ecology*. Englewood Cliffs, N.J.: Prentice-Hall, 1969.

Malthus, Thomas Robert. *An Essay on the Principle of Population as It Affects the Future Improvement of Society*. London: Johnson, 1798.

Odum, Eugene P. *Fundamentals of Ecology*. Philadelphia: Saunders, 1959.

Saylor, J. Gaylord & William M. Alexander. *Curriculum Planning for Modern Schools*. New York: Holt, Rinehart and Winston, 1966.

Shafer, Elwood L., Jr. "Perception of Natural Environments," in *Environment and Behavior*. Beverly Hills, Calif.: Sage, 1969, pp. 71–82.

Shelford, Victor E. *The Ecology of North America*, Urbana: University of Illinois Press, 1963.

Turesson, G. "The Species and the Variety as Ecological Units," *Hereditas*, 3:100–113, 1922.

chapter 3 / the learner and environmental education

A thorough understanding of the teaching and learning processes and the principles of human development is essential for a teacher who desires to engage students in relevant, individualized environmental education. As he selects, plans, and implements such education for his students, he should try to take into account how children learn, so that his established goals can be achieved. In this chapter we shall review current information on all these points. Our focus will be on facilitating the development of independent learning in environmental education.

Sound environmental attitudes are more often "caught" than "taught." The school itself should be a model of an unlittered, unpolluted environment that affords children opportunities to participate actively in environmental citizenship. This kind of active engagement in problem solving in the real world, under the guidance of a competent teacher, provides experiences for which mere "listening" is a poor substitute.

UNDERSTANDING CHILDREN

Children are by nature fascinated with their environment: with plants, animals, rocks, and various man-made objects and processes. If we understand how children learn, we can effectively capitalize on this natural interest. As teachers we constantly tell ourselves that each child learns at different rates and in different ways, but our instructional practices often do not reflect this basic principle of educational psychology. Psychologists have also recognized a general learning process, the components of which are presented schematically in Figure 3.1.

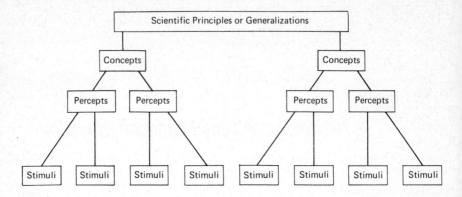

Figure 3.1   Learning ladder. From Arthur A. Carin and Robert B. Sund, *Teaching Science through Discovery*, 2d ed. (Columbus, Ohio: Charles E. Merrill Publishing Company, 1970). Chart modified from Charlotte Crabtree and Fannie Shaftel, "Fostering Thinking," *Curriculum for Today's Boys and Girls*, Robert S. Fleming, ed. (Columbus, Ohio: Charles E. Merrill Publishing Company, 1963).

The child learns about his environment through percepts. A percept is the impression of a stimulus obtained through the senses. Percepts combine with mental images, verbal symbols, and related input to form concepts. For example, the child learns the concept "dog" by feeling the animal's body, smelling its odor, hearing its bark, and seeing its wagging tail and other behavior.

Percepts can be learned. We tend to perceive what we have learned to perceive or even what we want to perceive. Early sensory experiences strongly influence later learning. The research of Piaget (1964) indicates that a child's ability to work with the broad concepts of space, time, matter, and causation depends upon a type of learning that evolves from his direct sensory experiences. A generalization, or principle, is a statement about the relations among concepts, abstractions, or objects.

Psychologist Robert M. Gagné has called conceptual learning the "acquisition of a common response," (1965, p. 189). Learning principles involves the combination of concepts and their applications. It seems likely that a child who clearly understands a principle will understand the concepts from which it has emerged.

Higgins (1962) has noted that the process of generalizing is essentially one of analysis, comparison, and discovering likenesses, differences, and connections. Isolated facts or concepts may seem insignificant, but in combination they may become useful. Principles do not remain eternally valid. We are living in an era of tremendous change, and generalizations about man and his environment are constantly subject to evaluation and revision.

As a child matures, he reconstructs previous learning at higher levels of abstraction. Research indicates that each child develops intellectually in stages from birth to postadolescence. For example, Piaget has demonstrated four major stages in the development of intelligence: sensory-motor, preoperational, concrete operational, and formal operational (Flavell, 1963).

The sensory-motor stage occurs in earliest infancy, as the human being acquires practical knowledge of his environment. Perceptions are very limited during this preverbal period, but the child does assimilate sensations through his own motor activities and what he sees, hears, touches, or otherwise senses.

The preoperational stage is characterized by the beginnings of language. During this period the child's judgments are based mainly on visual perceptions and are therefore frequently incorrect. For example, he thinks that an amount of liquid changes when it is poured from one container into another of a different shape or that a ball reshaped into a "hot dog" is larger.

During the concrete-operations stage the child learns to manipulate data about objects mentally. He develops ideas of number, space and time, and elementary logic.

The fourth stage of intellectual behavior is that of formal operations. Whereas before the child has tended to solve problems by emphasizing concrete aspects, he may now devise solutions without direct reference to perceptible objects.

According to Piaget, these stages are independent of chronological time; the most relevant point is sequence, rather than the age or length of time at any given stage of development. The knowledge of children required by the teacher is vast, and the skills for gathering and interpreting it are very complex. The following illustration indicates the necessary scope of understanding:

> This is the story of a classroom episode that could and does happen in just about the same way in numerous classrooms throughout the country: As Miss Cooper calls upon Jane to react to a question, she is disturbed (again) by Johnny who interrupts the session with his version of the answer that is completely off the subject and contrary to the class practice of breaking in upon another person's right to speak. The teacher is forced to deal with Johnny in the usual squelching way, but she is also becoming more aware that he must first be understood. She may ask the following questions to guide her thinking concerning his behavior to find out why he acts as he does:

1. Is he entering early adolescence? Could he be calling attention, as it were, to his growth?

2. Does he possess a high energy level or output?

3. Are major physical changes taking place, causing difficulty in accepting such changes?

4. Is there a lack of good interpersonal relationships with his family?

5. Is he competing? With his family?

6. Is he seeking a better interpersonal relationship with his family?

7. Does he have low status with his group? Is he striking back in the only way he knows?

8. Is this the beginning of an interest in the boy-girl relationship?

9. Does he come from a cultural pattern that encourages this kind of behavior?

10. Is the school expecting too much from him? Confusing him? Does he feel academically inferior? Bored?

11. Does his behavior suggest that this might be language experimentation?

12. Does he have an adequate self-concept of himself and of the adult he expects to be?

13. Is this his way of employing psychological weapons for ego support? (Morgan, 1957, p. 431)

HELPING CHILDREN TO SATISFY THEIR NEEDS

To help children satisfy their needs more effectively, we must understand how such needs are satisfied. Maslow (1943) has developed a hierarchy of human needs in the order of their importance to the individual: physiological needs, safety needs, needs for love and belonging, needs for esteem, needs for self-actualization, and needs to know and to understand.

Physiological needs include those for oxygen, food, warmth, and activity—all essential to maintenance of life. The very young child's behavior is particularly directed toward satisfying these needs. Safety needs include avoidance of various forms of perceived danger, preference for routine over disorder, and related stabilizing behavior. The child also needs affectionate relations with people. A strong desire to be accepted by the peer group exemplifies this need. Needs for esteem are met through recognition and acceptance by others. The satisfaction of these needs results in feelings of confidence and worth. Needs for self-actualization require the individual to realize his own potential, to "become somebody," in his own eyes. The needs to know and to understand are manifested in curiosity, exploration, and the quest for knowledge. The child's natural desire to explore his environment has already been emphasized in this chapter.

Maslow has emphasized that man is a perpetually "wanting" animal and that his needs must be satisfied in a particular sequence. That is, physiological needs must be met before a person can attend to satisfaction of his safety needs. As a certain class of needs is fairly well satisfied, the next higher class becomes more pressing (see Figure 3.2).

SYSTEMATIC INSTRUCTION

Too often teachers approach instruction haphazardly, leaving too many variables to chance. One of our problems is a tendency to ask the wrong questions. We ask "What shall I do?" or "What content must I get across?" instead of "What do I want my learner to become?" The difference can be formulated as between emphasis on means and goals (Popham & Baker, 1970). The means-oriented instructor is primarily concerned with "improving his techniques" and general classroom procedures. The goal-oriented instructor focuses initially upon what observable behavior he wishes the learner to exhibit at the conclusion of instruction. Having specified these goals, he then selects instructional means more easily and is generally more effective in instruction. In fact, his attention is on the learner instead of on himself.

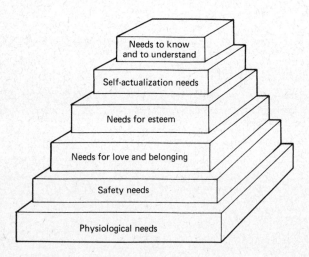

Figure 3.2 Hierarchy and prepotency of needs. From Marcella H. Nerbovig and Herbert J. Klausmeier, *Teaching in the Elementary School,* 3d ed. (New York: Harper & Row, Publishers, Inc., 1969). Based on data from pp. 80–93 in Abraham Maslow, *Motivation and Personality* (New York: Harper & Row, 1954).

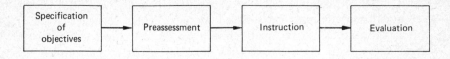

Figure 3.3 A goal-referenced instructional model. From W. James Popham and Eva L. Baker, *Systematic Instruction,* © 1970. By permission of Prentice-Hall, Inc.

One goal-oriented instructional model is presented in Figure 3.3. It emphasizes planning and assessment over teaching procedures:

1. The objectives of instruction are formulated in behavioral terms.
2. The learner is assessed in relation to the instructional objectives.
3. Instructional activities are designed to develop the goal behavior.
4. The student's progress relative to the specified objectives is evaluated.

In implementing this systematic approach to instruction the teacher can collect data on possible instructional improvements. If he has not succeeded in eliciting the goal behavior, he can evaluate each operation separately to identify the reason. Figure 3.4 illustrates the self-correction features of this instructional model.

Formulating Behavioral Goals

An instructional objective can be formulated as a statement of how the learner is to behave when he has successfully completed an instructional experience. An appropriate activity engages the student in practicing the goal behavior itself or one analogous to it. Here are five behavioral objectives, along with directly related and analogous activities and prerequisite skills:

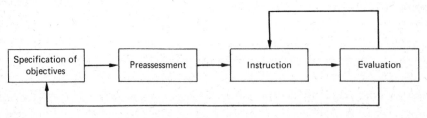

Figure 3.4 Courses of action dictated by evaluation of results. From W. James Popham and Eva L. Baker, *Systematic Instruction,* © 1970. By permission of Prentice-Hall, Inc.

I. *Objective.* To assemble a microscope from its elements.
  A. *Directly related activity.* To observe the assembly of a microscope by the instructor and then to practice it.
  B. *Analogous activity.* To discuss the steps and procedures necessary to assemble a microscope.
  C. *Prerequisite skills.*
    1. Recognition of the various parts of a microscope.
    2. Recognition of the functions of the various parts.
    3. Recognition of the interrelations of the parts.
    4. Manual ability to assemble the parts.
II. *Objective.* To list in order the seven prescribed steps in proper microscope operation.
  A. *Directly related activity.* To list in order the seven pre-scribed steps in proper microscope operation.
  B. *Analogous activity.* To describe orally the seven steps of proper microscope operation.
  C. *Prerequisite skills.*
    1. Recognition of the steps in microscope operation.
    2. Ability to spell and to write.
III. *Objective.* To apply in order the seven prescribed steps in proper microscope operation.
  A. *Directly related activity.* Manual operation of the microscope, from the first step through the seventh step.
  B. *Analogous activity.* To write the seven prescribed steps of proper microscope operation in order.
  C. *Prerequisite skills.*
    1. Ability to manipulate microscope controls.
    2. Recognition of microscope parts designated in prescribed steps.
    3. Recognition of the functions of the various parts of the microscope.
IV. *Objective.* To describe orally five distinguishing characteristics of an amoeba as seen through the microscope.
  A. *Directly related activity.* To discuss the five basic distinguishing characteristics of an amoeba while observing it through a microscope.
  B. *Analogous activity.* To watch slides of an amoeba and to listen to the instructor describe its five distinguishing characteristics.
  C. *Prerequisite skills.*
    1. Cognitive recognition of the terms used to describe the basic characteristics of an amoeba.

        2. Ability to see the amoeba through the microscope, including ability to use the microscope.

        3. Oral description of the characteristics of an amoeba.

V. *Objective.* To draw an amoeba, labeling the five basic distinguishing characteristics as diagramed and labeled in the textbook.

  A. *Directly related activity.* To practice drawing and labeling the basic characteristics of an amoeba by referring to the labeled diagram of the amoeba in the textbook.

  B. *Analogous activity.* To observe the instructor drawing and labeling an amoeba as he explains the labeled diagram in the textbook.

  C. *Prerequisite skills.*

    1. Drawing the amoeba.

    2. Writing.

    3. Recognizing the application of labels to the characteristics of the amoeba.

    4. Reading and interpreting the labeled diagram in the textbook.

Criteria for Instructional Goals

Teachers can improve their instructional objectives by applying three main criteria. First, is the objective stated in concise *behavioral* terms? Does it describe the specific observable behavior in which the learner is to engage or what he is to produce? An objective must be clearly defined so that the learner can understand the kind of performance that will be acceptable as evidence of achievement. (For assistance in the application of this criterion, see Mager, 1962.)

    Is the objective *appropriate* to the learner? Is it too difficult or too easy? Is it relevant to his life and environment? Is it worthwhile? In selecting appropriate instructional objectives the teacher may rely on his own values and taxonomic analysis. The teacher's own framework of values is most important in deciding what his students should learn. Elementary-school teachers may have strong commitments to certain kinds of learning; this commitment is important but should be kept in proper perspective. The teacher should remember that his values may be significantly different from those held by many of his students.

    The taxonomies of educational objectives developed by Bloom (1956) and his associates (Krathwohl *et al.*, 1964) may be particularly helpful in planning appropriate goals. After extensive research they classified the many objectives that they had tested in schools in three "domains": cognitive, affective, and psychomotor. Cognitive objectives include acquisition of knowledge and use of this knowledge in carrying out tasks or solving problems. Affective objectives include acquisition of attitudinal, emotional, and evaluative responses. The psychomotor objectives include acquisition of manipulative skills.

An analysis of instructional objectives common in American schools has revealed that affective objectives are seriously neglected. Because many teachers probably overemphasize the cognitive domain without realizing it, application of taxonomic analysis should help them to plan more appropriate instructional objectives.

What *level* of performance is expected? What evidence indicates that the learner has achieved it? Under what conditions should he be able to achieve it? A well-formulated objective should cover at least three points: what the student is to be able to do, under what conditions he will be expected to do it, and to what degree will he be expected to do it (should he be able to solve 50 percent, 80 percent, or 90 percent of the problems?). In addition to establishing minimum performance levels for individuals, the teacher should establish such levels for the class as a whole. If 60 percent of the students solve 60 percent of the problems incorrectly, then either the teacher is asking the wrong questions, or something is wrong with the entire instructional program.

As an example of a formulation of the conditions under which the student will be expected to perform, we might offer this statement: "Given ten pairs of short poems, one of each pair being a selection by Carl Sandburg and the other by a different author, the student should be able to choose, with at least 90 percent accuracy, the ten selections written by Sandburg."

The specified level of performance is "at least 90 percent accuracy." The conditions are "given ten pairs" and the selection of the poems "written by Sandburg."

There is a definite relationship between the clarity of a teacher's goals and his effectiveness. Careful attention to the various components of an instructional model should increase that effectiveness.

INDIVIDUALIZED INSTRUCTION

Mitzel (1970) has distinguished between "independent study" and "individualized instruction." Independent study involves study in isolation from other learners. Individualized instruction is the tailoring of the scope, sequence, and time of instruction to individuals within a group setting. It emphasizes an appropriate level of content and experience for each learner.

Let us briefly review four conceptions of individualization. First is allowing the learner to proceed through materials at his own pace. Second is allowing him to work at times that he chooses. Third is beginning his instruction at a point appropriate to his previous achievement. Fourth is furnishing the learner with a great variety of instructional media from which he may select.

Several instructional approaches incorporate some or all of these four notions of individualization. They include "inquiry teaching," "non-gradedness," use of paraprofessionals, flexible grouping, and the "learning-activity package."

"Inquiry Teaching"

Teaching through inquiry is based on helping the student to learn how to learn. The approach emphasizes the student's motivation, knowledge, and mental health and aims at helping him to redirect his behavior toward goals that he values. In contrast, expository teaching permits the student little or no autonomy in the learning process. Inquiry teaching thus encourages broad student participation and the expression of divergent points of view. As students try to answer questions about man and his environment, they begin to grasp that knowledge is provisional, rather than absolute.

In "inquiry teaching" the instructor must fulfill various roles:

1. *Planner.* He must plan learning activities according to individual needs, collect and prepare suitable materials, and schedule the sequence and time intervals for them.
2. *Introducer.* It is most important to introduce each specific learning experience at the appropriate time and in a manner that generates additional inquiry.
3. *Sustainer.* Through a pattern of questioning, the teacher strives to involve students in exploring alternatives and validating responses by means of available data. He emphasizes critical thinking and difference of opinion, rather than imposing his own ideas.
4. *Manager.* As executive of the learning environment, the teacher uses all available concepts, techniques, and resources to involve students in planning and implementing inquiries on their own. This involves the arrangement of the learning environment, supervising teacher aides, and selecting and utilizing material resources effectively.
5. *Rewarder.* The teacher rewards creative and imaginative work. He suggests, praises, and encourages students to "play their hunches" in exploring approaches to solving problems.
6. *Value Investigator.* The teacher must very seriously consider the student's affective learning. We should help the student to develop

a system of evaluation in which various points of view are recognized so that the pupil can most effectively develop his own values. (Massialas, 1969, p. 44)

A major task for the teacher is to ensure that children have many opportunities to engage in many types of carefully planned scientific inquiry about their natural and social environment:

1. *Observation.* The child learns to ask: "What am I looking for? What am I looking at? What do I see?" He should be encouraged to think about what he has observed, to ask questions, to make predictions, and to arrive at tentative conclusions.
2. *Measurement.* This operation teaches the child precision in his observations and predictions. He should be trained in various types of measurement: of area, volume, length, and weight, for example.
3. *Experimentation.* When the child manipulates an object or objects to observe change, he is experimenting. Through such controlled encounters, he learns to move beyond the realm of guesswork.
4. *Description.* This procedure trains the child to communicate ideas about properties like color, size, shape, texture, taste, and classification of objects. He must also learn to describe functions accurately.
5. *Generalization.* Observation, description, and classification permit statements applicable to categories broader than the actual samples studied.
6. *Deduction.* Through reasoning the child learns when hypotheses can be either confirmed or rejected and how to base predictions on his conclusions (Frost & Rowland, 1969).

While practicing these and related scientific operations, the child must explore the structures of the natural and social sciences. Structure is the body of concepts and principles; process is the methods by which scientists discover or impose structure. The study of structure and process should constitute the "fiber" of the environmental-education program in the elementary school.

Purposeful activity, verbalization, and discovery help the learner to generalize. Students cannot develop such skills in a silent, stifling classroom, where exploratory discussions are rare. The teacher has a tremendous responsibility to provide an atmosphere conducive to inquiry and to lead the students toward desired goals.

"Nongradedness"

"Nongradedness" embodies a philosophy, a way of viewing the educational process, that emphasizes individualized instruction. It involves a vertical organization of the school in which pupils progress at their own individual rates. Each must complete as much of an appropriate curriculum as he can, but promotion and retention are eliminated. There are many specific models of school organization, but Goodlad (1963) has outlined the assumptions basic to any "nongraded" model:

1. Schools are centered on learners.
2. The focus is on helping students to develop *ways* of knowing and thinking.
3. Grouping patterns are flexible, and individual differences are accommodated through "intraclass," rather than through "interclass," arrangements—that is, by using a variety of grouping provisions within the class (ability, achievement, interest, multi-age, pupil teams) and by providing for individualization within the class as opposed to juggling from class to class.
4. Variations in development are recognized and incorporated into individualized programs.
5. Provision is made for differentiated programs based on differential rates of progress. The emphasis in reporting progress is on how well each student is fulfilling his own potential.

"Nongrading" thus focuses on continuous progress by each pupil, rather than on content or standardized achievement. It does not matter what kinds of groupings (content, interage, ability, and so on) are used, the essential idea is that teachers' common notions of grading, grouping, normal progress, "passing," and "failing" are abolished. "Nongrading" involves recognition that each child has idiosyncratic goals, drives, values, and intellectual and operational equipment. Teachers must cease to think in terms of homogeneous achievement and grade-level content.

The Changing Role of the Teacher

Significant changes in what is expected of elementary-school teachers continually occur. Although teachers were once regarded simply as the major classroom source of information and instiller of the three "R"s, today they are expected to fulfill many if not all of the following roles:

1. A diagnostician, who carefully analyzes students' aptitudes and achievements before guiding them into new learning experiences.

2. One among many sources of information.
3. A human-development specialist, who plans learning experiences according to sound principles of growth, development, and learning.
4. A programmer of behavioral change, who helps each student to develop desirable behavior within the affective, cognitive, and psychomotor domains.
5. An executive, who makes significant decisions about the appropriate involvement of the learner with human and material resources (particularly media and paraprofessionals) within the learning environment.
6. A team member, who cooperates with other professionals in planning and teaching.
7. An evaluator of student programs, who assesses and reports each student's progress in terms of his own capabilities.
8. An identity model, who facilitates the positive development of the student's personality and self-concept.
9. A curriculum and instruction strategist, who tests the effectiveness of instructional materials and is expert in planning individualized experiences for students.
10. An inquiry agent, a master teacher, who helps the student to clarify, internalize, and apply facts, concepts, and processes.
11. A specialist in particular subject matter.
12. A source of guidance, who assists children to solve individual problems.
13. A public-relations and communications specialist, who can interpret the school program to all segments of the larger society.
14. A clerk and custodian.
15. A friend, a source of help and inspiration when the child feels forsaken.

In addition to performing these roles, most elementary-school teachers are expected to teach several subject areas with very little, if any, time during the school day for instructional planning. No teacher is "just a teacher." Each is, as a result of individual traits and professional preparation, more effective in some roles than in others. Each teacher must choose his own priorities, emphasizing those functions that make the greatest positive difference in the lives of children. It is most important that differentiated staffing models be tailored to individual schools, according to students' needs and teachers' characteristics. Differentiated staffing means assigning teachers on the basis of matching their various combinations and degrees of talent to children's needs. Each teacher should devote most of his time and energies to doing what he does best.

Use of Paraprofessionals

The effective use of paraprofessional staff, or aides, may contribute significantly to individualized instruction. An aide is an adult who assists or supports in the school program under the direction of professionals. Self has suggested ways in which an aide can help a child:

> Aides can help a child's development unfold, can help develop a child's curiosity, allow a child to make many choices and decisions and small mistakes, help a child feel special and unique, help a child to develop his imagination and self-expression, foster a child's emotional development, permit a child to develop close feelings of trust toward adults, school personnel and other figures of authority, and aides can truly teach. (Self, 1968, p. 18)

Three basic types of aides are employed in schools: instructional, administrative and clerical, and community and social-service aides.

Instructional aides assist the teacher in the learning setting. They range from older children who work with younger children, through adults with less than high-school training and adults with some college training, to college interns and student teachers. The kinds of tasks that such aides perform should be determined by their own competence and student needs. The primary reason for using aides is to free teachers to perform the professional functions for which they are uniquely qualified by training and experience. Great care in selecting and assigning aides is necessary. Some states have developed policies for the use of aides. New Jersey (*Regulations and Recommendations*, 1968) is a leader in this area. Policies on certification; standards for appointment, assignment, and supervision; and preservice and in-service training have been developed.

Administrative and clerical aides may perform some of the following functions:

1. Assisting in development of positive relations between home and school.
2. Working with attendance problems, especially making home visits.
3. Assisting in the development of effective home-study habits.
4. Assisting sick or injured children by obtaining the services of a nurse or doctor, notifying parents, performing minor first aid, and so on.
5. Assisting individual children with particular problems.
6. Serving as models of success.

Community and social service aides may perform the following functions:

1. Providing a liaison between school personnel and the community health and welfare agencies.
2. Performing community relations activities.
3. Working with parents on chronic attendance problems.
4. Interpreting to school personnel the needs, anxieties, and conflicts of the parents.

When aides are drawn from ethnic or economic backgrounds similar to those of the children, they may be able to open channels of communication inaccessible to the regular school staff. The effective use of aides may facilitate development of more individualized instructional programs.

According to Hymes (1968), no matter who the aide is, a program is improved when more than one mind, more than one set of eyes and ears, and more than one pair of hands and feet are present. He is fully committed to the idea that every teacher must have a helper.

Flexible Grouping

More varied instructional groupings—larger and smaller classes, longer and shorter class periods, meetings of various frequency—all facilitate independent learning. Grouping has always been a perplexing problem in the elementary school. Shane (1960) has cited ten major difficulties in the development of educationally sound grouping practices: lack of specific and valid data on individual children; mobility of students; uneven, continuously changing growth patterns of children; variation in the philosophy, experience, and competence of teachers; maturity and competence of administrative leaders; curriculum characteristics; policies on selection and use of instructional materials; size of the elementary school; and the availability of appropriate personnel resources. In addition, he has provided a survey of thirty-two grouping plans used in the United States over the past century.

A careful review of the potpourri of educational research on grouping will probably leave the reviewer still more perplexed. Very few significant findings or new approaches have been revealed during the past five years. A study reported by Yerkovich (1968) yielded some most interesting data on grouping students by somatotype for reading instruction. Students were grouped according to three body types: endomorph, mesomorph, and ectomorph. From achievement-test scores, Yerkovich concluded that, compared to traditional grouping patterns, this type of homogeneous grouping produced significant gains in student achievement.

A poll of teachers' opinions ("Teacher Opinion Poll," 1968) on ability grouping was conducted by the National Education Association Research Division. A scientifically selected sample of the nation's public-school teachers was asked what types of pupils (defined by ability) they would prefer to teach. Forty-two percent preferred "average" ability, and 26 percent preferred high ability. Only 3 percent indicated preference for the low-ability group.

There is no single best grouping pattern. The "best" pattern is the one that facilitates optimum learning for each pupil in the specific school. But all grouping should be based on reliable data, multiple criteria, and flexibility in movement from group to group.

The Learning-Activity Package

To provide each student with alternatives for what, how, when, and where to learn; to strengthen pupil-teacher communications; and to use a wide range of learning resources, a new dimension in instructional planning and organization is required. One example is the learning-activity package (LAP), in which the student is given far greater opportunity and responsibity to learn on his own (see Figures 3.5 and 3.6).

I. General Information
   Name: _____
   Age: _____
   Grade level: _____

II. Test Data
   Mental Age: _____
   Achievement: (indicate test, data, date)
   1. Reading
   2. Math
   3. Language Arts
   4. Science
   5. Social Studies
   6. Health and Physical Education
   7. Creative Arts
   8. Others
III. Health Data
IV. Home Background
 V. Interests
VI. Attitudes
VII. Additional information

Figure 3.5. Pupil data profile.

I. Title, type learner
II. Brief overview—Directions
III. Pretest
IV. Behavioral objectives
   Upon completion of this unit, you should be able to:
   1.
   2.
   3.
   4.
V. Required activities
   During this unit you are to do the following activities:
   1.
   2.
   3.
   4.
   5.
   6. Take the post test
VI. Teacher check points
VII. Student evaluation techniques
VIII. Optional activities
IX. Post test

Figure 3.6. Learning activity package outline.

Each package is developed by the teacher to lead the student through a series of programmed educational experiences relevant to his interests and goals at a particular time. Although the specific format of an LAP may vary according to students' needs, one workable format devised at Nova High School in Nova, Florida, included the following components: rationale, performance objectives, pretest, pretest analysis, basic references, program for learning, self-evaluation test and analysis, and appendix (including references, glossary, related problems, and projects; Arena, 1970).

One specific goal of most teachers is to help students to assume greater responsibility for their own learning. Each LAP includes several intervals in which the learner must decide the content that he will study, the media activities in which he will engage, and the mode of instruction that he will receive. He may choose to read, to view films or filmstrips, to engage in nature study, to listen to tapes, and so on. The teacher is available for consultation but not as a crutch. Each package is based on self-pacing and self-assessment, in addition to evaluation by the teacher. A student progresses through learning activities at his own rate, beginning at a level of sophistication appropriate to his ability. Learning experiences can be tailored to slower, brighter, and home-bound students, for example. A school does not have to develop a totally individualized instructional program in order to use the LAP approach effectively. The approach may be used as an alternative or supplement to conventional ones.

The teacher who follows a LAP is primarily a planner of learning activities and a resource for students. In order to enhance his role, he must renounce emphasis on lecturing, use of the textbook as primary source material, uniformity of content for all students, and reliance on fifty-minute class periods.

The reader should note our emphasis on "teacher-made" instructional packages. Commercially developed packages of every kind are now flooding the market; a teacher who understands the philosophy and procedures involved in the design and use of the LAP is in a much better position to select from packages on the market. The wholesale adoption and blind implementation of commercially prepared packages can be disastrous. The advantages of the LAP approach lie in its emphasis on sound individualized instruction.

SUMMARY

To facilitate independent learning in environmental education, we must rely on systematic and effective instructional principles and practices. A thorough understanding of how children develop mentally, physically, and socially is basic. A goal-oriented instructional model assists the teacher in refining the learning process.

Increased understanding and application of "inquiry teaching," associated with various approaches to individualized instruction, will enable the teacher to provide more relevant environmental education for children. Instruction should become increasingly more personal, emphasizing the development of independent learning.

INVESTIGATIONS

1. Conduct a survey of your school building and grounds. To what degree do they represent a model of an unlittered, unpolluted environment? List specific features. What action is necessary to improve the model significantly?

2. Study the work of Piaget (1964). Which of his specific findings should the teacher apply in environmental education? (See Chittenden, 1970; Baldwin, *Theories of Child Development* [New York: Wiley, 1967]; and Piaget, 1964.)

3. Carefully review Popham and Baker's work (1970). Develop two lesson plans for environmental instruction, one emphasizing means

and the other goals. What are the implications of each for the learner and the teacher?

4. Develop and teach an environmental lesson plan in an elementary school. Carefully evaluate your role in terms of Massialas' six "inquiry teaching" functions (1969). Which functions did you perform most effectively? Least effectively? Why?

5. Carefully review Maslow's hierarchy of human needs (1943). Maslow has emphasized that man is a perpetually "wanting" animal and that his needs must be satisfied in a particular sequence. What are the implications of this comment for man's relation to his environment?

6. Read Arena's article on individualizing instruction (1970), which includes an excellent treatment of the LAP. Diagnose a learner and prepare a LAP for his environmental education.

7. Visit a local elementary-school media center or library. Identify instructional materials pertinent to environmental education. Discuss with the librarian his role in facilitating an environmental-education program. After additional research return to him with suggestions for improving the selection of environmental-education materials.

REFERENCES

Arena, John E. "An Instrument for Individualizing Instruction," *Educational Leadership*, 27:784–787, May 1970.

Bloom, Benjamin S. (ed.). *Taxonomy of Educational Objectives. Handbook I: Cognitive Domain.* New York: McKay, 1956.

Carin, Arthur A. & Robert B. Sund. *Teaching Science through Discovery*, 2nd ed. Columbus, Ohio: Merrill, 1970.

Chittenden, Edward A. "Piaget and Elementary Science," *Science and Children*, 8:9–15, December 1970.

Flavell, John H. *The Developmental Psychology of Jean Piaget.* Princeton, N.J.: Van Nostrand, 1963.

Frost, Joe L. & G. Thomas Rowland. *Curricula for the Seventies.* Boston: Houghton Mifflin, 1969.

Gagné, Robert M. "The Learning of Concepts," *School Review*, 73:187–196, Autumn 1965.

Goodlad, John I. *Planning and Organizing for Teaching.* Washington, D.C.: National Education Association, 1963.

Higgins, J. M. "New Viewpoints in the Social Studies," *Canadian Education and Research Digest*, 2:252, December 1962.

Hymes, James L., Jr. "More Help for Teachers," in *Aides to Teachers and Children*, Bulletin 24-A. Washington, D.C.: Association for Supervision and Curriculum Development, National Education Association, 1968.

Krathwohl, David R., Benjamin S. Bloom & Bertran B. Masis. *Taxonomy of Educational Objectives. Handbook II: Affective Domain.* New York: McKay, 1964.

Mager, Robert. *Preparing Instructional Objectives.* Palo Alto, Calif.: Fearon, 1962.

Maslow, A. H. "A Theory of Human Motivation," *Psychological Review,* 50:370–396, 1943.

Massialas, Byron G. "Inquiry," *Today's Education,* 58:40–42, May 1969.

Mitzel, Harold E. "The Impending Instruction Revolution," *Phi Delta Kappan,* 51:434–439, April 1970.

Morgan, H. G. "Toward Understanding Children," *Education,* 77:430–434, March 1957.

Nerbovig, Marcella H. & Herbert J. Klausmeier. *Teaching in the Elementary School.* New York: Harper, 1969.

Piaget, Jean. "Development and Learning," *Journal of Research in Science Teaching,* 2:176–185, 1964.

Popham, W. James & Eva I. Baker. *Systematic Instruction.* Englewood Cliffs, N.J.: Prentice-Hall, 1970.

Regulations and Recommendations of the State Board of Education for the Employment, Assignment, Supervision, and Training of School Aides, Trenton: New Jersey Office of Teacher Education and Certification, 1968.

Self, Frank. "Finding and Using Aides," in *Aides to Teachers and Children,* Bulletin 24-A. Washington, D.C.: Association for Supervision and Curriculum Development, National Education Association, 1968.

Shane, Harold G. "Grouping in the Elementary School," *Phi Delta Kappan,* 41:313–319, April 1960.

"Teacher Opinion Poll—Ability Grouping," *NEA Journal,* 57:53, February 1968.

Yerkovich, Raymond J. "Somatotypes: A New Method in Grouping," *Clearing House,* 42:278–279, January 1968.

chapter 4 / designing the environmental-education curriculum

The elementary school should provide a model in which children can learn positive attitudes and practices toward the environment. It should help children develop through direct experience responsibility for and appreciation of environmental maintenance and improvement. The development and application of environmental-education curricula is one of the most urgent needs of the 1970s. As President Richard M. Nixon said in his 1970 State of the Union message: "The great question of the 70's is, shall we surrender to our surroundings or shall we make our peace with nature and begin to make reparations for the damage we have done to our air, to our land, to water?" (*Congressional Record*, p. H187.) John Fischer (1969, p. 14) has proposed that the concept of survival become the organizing principle for many fields of scholarly inquiry. Education for survival could be an organizing focal point for curriculum development from the kindergarten through the university.

ENVIRONMENTAL GOALS

The Task Force on Environmental Health and Related Problems of the U.S. Department of Health, Education, and Welfare (1967) has identified ten goals for mastering environmental threats to man's health and welfare:

1. Restoration of air quality, emphasizing reduction of plant-stack and vehicle-exhaust emission.
2. A program of testing existing and proposed public drinking-water supply systems and enforcement of water standards.

3. A waste-disposal program, including research and development.
4. Population research to determine the effects of population trends on preservation of the environment.
5. An effort to discover levels of human tolerance of the massive pressures of the urban environment.
6. Establishment of standards for synthetic materials, trace elements, and chemicals.
7. A consumer-protection agency to identify and control hazards to consumer health.
8. Control of radiation and protection of the public from its effects.
9. A program for prevention of occupational diseases and accidents.
10. A government program, emphasizing voluntary compliance, for appropriate housing, transportation, and urban development.

These national goals have already generated some far-reaching measures to improve the quality of the environment. The Environmental Education Act was designed to promote environmental education at all levels by providing funds for curriculum development and personnel. The Act, which became law when President Nixon signed it on October 30, 1970, provided two million dollars in start-up funds for the first fiscal year with progressively higher funds planned for future years. This has provided an impetus for significant curriculum development in environmental education on a nation-wide basis. (A summary of the Act may be found in *Environment and the Schools, a Special Report by the Editors of Education, U.S.A.* [Washington, D.C.: National School Public Relations Association, 1971].)

Coordination of efforts at all levels is especially important: Local school personnel should work closely with state personnel in organizing and conducting environmental-education conferences and workshops, developing materials, and designing curricula.

The environmental-education curriculum in the elementary school should be directed toward producing citizens who understand the biophysical environment and problems related to it, have ideas of how to help solve these problems, and are motivated to positive action. The biophysical environment includes both natural and man-made components.

PUBLIC SUPPORT FOR ENVIRONMENTAL EDUCATION

Generally speaking, public education reflects the support that it receives from the community, and it is rarely stronger than the people's interest in it and their willingness to fund it. It therefore follows that, if environmental education is to become a functional part of the public schools, all available publicity and educational media should be used to stimulate interest in and desire for the program. The Conservation Education Association, Inc., has developed a plan for environmental studies on a state-wide basis, including roles for state superintendents of public instruction, all school personnel, and lay advisory committees.

Wilhelmina Hill (1970), Coordinator for Environmental Education of the U.S. Office of Education, has suggested the formation of state and local committees of teachers, school administrators, women's clubs, service groups, youth groups, churches, community planners, and related groups to

1. Formulate and recommend statewide policies on curriculum development, standards of instruction, teacher preparation, and evaluation of materials in environmental education.
2. Encourage sympathy for the goals of environmental education, especially among school administrators.
3. Use all available resources to provide the schools with materials and other aids for students in environmental studies.
4. Guide budgeting of available funds so that environmental-education expenditures can achieve maximum results.

MAJOR CURRICULUM OBJECTIVES

Training concerned citizens who can contribute to improving environmental quality should be a major function of our schools. It should be accomplished through a comprehensive curriculum extending from kindergarten through the university. It is especially imperative that we confront the problems of environmental ignorance and insensitivity during the formative years.

The major objectives of environmental education in the elementary school should be, first, to help the individuals acquire an understanding of the biophysical environment and society's relation to it. This understanding should include knowledge of the characteristics, distribution, interrelations, and uses of natural resources. Instruction in environmental engineering should emphasize striving for quality to improve human welfare.

The second major objective is to encourage understanding of man as an inseparable part of his environment but with the ability to alter it in important ways through his activity or lack of it. Especially critical is man's systematic interaction with the biophysical environment to advance human welfare.

A third objective is to generate understanding of the organizational strategies and social arrangements through which man interacts with the biophysical environment. Such understanding results from study of various political, legal, managerial, technical, and educational means by which man interacts with the environment and creates "environmental futures."

GUIDELINES FOR CURRICULUM DEVELOPMENT

We can suggest nine guidelines for the development of an environmental-education curriculum in the elementary school.

Environmental education should be designed in accordance with children's developmental stages. The preoperational, concrete-operations, and formal-operations stages posited by Piaget might serve as reference points. Experiences should be designed to facilitate the child's perception of his world through all his senses.

The curriculum design should incorporate concepts and processes from the natural (physical) and social sciences. Teaching basic principles of ecology is not enough; we must help students to appreciate their environment and to develop values that will guide positive action.

The core of the curriculum should be recognition of man's interdependence with both the natural and man-made components of his environment. Helping students to see themselves as interdependent with, rather than plundering masters of, their environment is crucial.

Environmental education should be an integral component of the curriculum and not simply an appendage "tacked on" to the existing curriculum. Previous efforts in this direction have been limited primarily to "conservation education" or "outdoor education." Although such instruction has merit, it is limited in scope and is often treated as an appendage to the central curriculum. Environmental education can become integral to the curriculum by either completely altering the existing curricular framework or extending existing programs. It is possible, for instance, to revise traditional programs of science and social studies to include appropriate environmental education.

Appropriate emphasis should be given to the study of natural, social, and man-made environments, especially their interrelations. The natural environment comprises the biotic world, the social environment is the network of relations among men, and the man-made environment consists of man's concrete modifications or structuring of the physical environment. Too often we have failed to help pupils understand the interrelations among these three and have taught instead only a limited conception of the natural environment.

The process of inquiry should be a prime vehicle for involving pupils in environmental studies. Too much schooling today consists of irrelevant paper-and-pencil exercises dictated by teachers. We must engage pupils in firsthand experiences that will have genuine meaning for them, and we must value students' questions as much as we value their answers. The school, school grounds, and overall community should serve as an "environmental laboratory" in which "children learn what they live."

Appropriate attention should be given to cognitive, affective, and psychomotor achievement. If one domain is to be emphasized, it should be the oft-neglected affective domain. Pupils need to develop systems of value analysis that will guide positive action related to the environment. All of us need a "science of humanity" through which man can interpret his world, find the best way to live in it, and contribute to betterment for all mankind.

The program should be planned on a continuum extending from kindergarten through the university. Environmental studies should have both continuity and sequence, with emphasis on related principles, concepts, and processes, rather than on apparently unrelated facts.

Provision should be made for in-service training of both professional and paraprofessional personnel. It is especially important to draw upon local citizens and local, state, and regional experts in environmental problems. We must develop partnerships in designing experiences for pupils. With the possible exception of some formal university study of ecology and related sciences, training programs can best be conducted, with a variety of human and material resources, at the local level.

Provisions for continuous evaluative feedback should be built into the program. This feedback should include data from pupils, patrons, and school personnel on how to achieve ever-greater improvement (Sale, 1970).

INTERDISCIPLINARY DESIGN

The type of curriculum design can have great influence on the quality of learning. A separate-subject approach often provides a very fragmented pattern of information for the learner, with few clues to what is most significant. The White House Office of Science and Technology (Carter, 1969) has emphasized the need for an interdisciplinary approach to environmental education. The report recommended that such an approach in universities encompass various "schools of the human environment." Departments within universities are being urged to combine their resources to develop new programs and to provide financial aid for students who elect them.

Our national environmental problems are not simply technical ones. They are social as well, arising directly out of human interaction within the total environment. If we are to develop new attitudes toward human survival and techniques to ensure it, the social sciences and the humanities must share the leadership. The humanities should involve basic questions about man and about knowing, from the mystic to the formalistic—with specific emphasis upon questions of valuing that enhance one's sensitivity to the environment.

Margaret Mead, distinguished anthropologist and a director of the American Museum of Natural History in New York, has insisted that continuing environmental education in all schools be the keystone of our effort to save the nation's natural heritage ("Congress," 1970). She has also recognized that interdisciplinary approaches are essential to good environmental education. The curriculum should not be limited to water and air pollution but should include much broader treatment of man as part of nature, the quality of life in the inner city and in every facet of society, "aesthetic" pollution, and comprehensive study of the biophysical environment.

Hare (1970) believes that the study of environmental problems must be interdisciplinary in a special sense. Rather than simply combining old disciplines, he argues that we must synthesize a new one. Long-term design and control of the environment are preferable to short-term correction of technological errors and "pollution control" gimmicks.

The social and natural sciences may be approached from an ecological point of view. Baker (1962) has cited three reasons why ecological theory may be important to anthropology: Ecology provides a body of theory developed from animal and plant studies that can be tested on man; it provides a frame of reference to remind us that man's biology, his culture, and his physical environment are not isolated from one another and that all are interrelated; and it provides an escape from the old "chicken and egg," cause-and-effect controversies that plague various areas of anthropology.

Edgerton's study (1965) of the values, attitudes, and tribal character of four African tribes of farmers and herders has strongly confirmed the usefulness of an interdisciplinary approach to environmental studies. It has yielded valuable findings about interrelations of culture and ecology. The farmers valued hard work, whereas the herders did not. The farmers tended to be "loners," abstract in their thinking, given to fantasy, and less able to control their emotions. The herders were direct, more willing to discuss the nitty-gritty problems and issues, rooted in reality, and more in control of their emotions. The farmers were also considerably more hostile than were the herders. These findings illustrate the ways in which physical environment influences economic adjustments in whole communities. These adjustments in turn affect personality, attitudes, values, and social organization.

A Correlation Model

Correlation of social studies and science is one possible basis for an environmental-education program. In developing a program for the Ann

Arbor, Michigan, public schools, Stapp (1965) used the following procedures:

I. Designing the Program
   A. Establishing a set of guiding principles that should be included in a conservation-education program.
   B. Examining the science and social-studies programs and identifying relevant elements in the existing curriculum.
   C. Developing themes for each elementary-grade level that would link the contents of the existing science and social-studies curricula and would provide continuity and progression in the program.
   D. Selecting conservation topics to be integrated into secondary-school science and social-studies courses.
   E. Developing an organization to facilitate integration of conservation education into the existing framework of the Ann Arbor public schools.

II. Preparation of Materials
   A. Preparing content on the theme developed for each elementary grade.
   B. Preparing content on each of the conservation topics selected by secondary-school science and social-studies teachers for integration into their courses.
   C. Designing charts for each elementary grade to help prepare learners for field trips.
   D. Constructing of a series of color slides to enhance classroom presentation of each conservation topic to be integrated into the secondary-school science and social-studies program.

III. Preparation of Teachers
   A. Providing in-service training workshops for elementary- and secondary-school teachers.
   B. Providing elementary- and secondary-school teachers with information on current conservation issues, in addition to the substantive material mentioned in II.

IV. Evaluation of the Program
   A. Sending open-ended qualitative-evaluation questionnaires to administrators (the superintendent of schools, the assistant superintendent in charge of curriculum, the social-studies coordinator, the science coordinator, and elementary- and secondary-school principals) and classroom teachers (secondary-school social-studies and science teachers and all elementary-school teachers). The recipients were asked to recall and record briefly the features of the conservation

program that they had thought helpful in working toward
the instructional goals of the Ann Arbor school system.
B. Sending quantitative-evaluation questionnaires to the same
group of teachers after all qualitative evaluations had been
returned. One series of questions was to be answered by
scoring on ten-point ungraded scales. Additional questions
were directed at uncovering new kinds of attitudes and
interests observed in students as a result of the program
and at gathering information on ways to improve it.

Modified Separate-Subject Designs

A modified separate-subject design might be used during the evolution of
a full-fledged environmental-education program (see Figure 4.1). This involves a transition toward an interdisciplinary design, an attempt to begin
to interrelate two or more disciplines to aid students in the transfer of
learning.

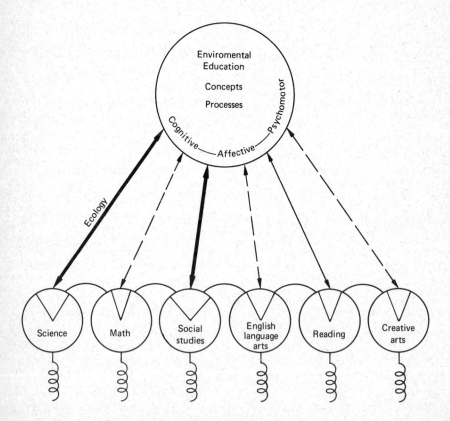

Figure 4.1 Modified separate subject design.

Other Interdisciplinary Designs

A full-fledged interdisciplinary design is a more desirable long-term alternative than is a modified separate-subject design. The reader may find an excellent example of an interdisciplinary environmental-education curriculum as it is presented in *Man: A Course of Study*. It was developed for older elementary-school and middle-school children by Bruner (1965) under the sponsorship of the Social Studies Curriculum Program of the Education Development Center, Inc., with grants from the National Science Foundation. It focuses on man's interrelations with the environment. The conceptual framework is based on Bruner's classification of the five "massive contributors to man's humanization": tool making, language, social organization, the management of his prolonged childhood, and his urge to explain his world. Bruner has emphasized that children need experiences through which they can learn in what ways man is unique in his adaptation to the world and to discern the continuity between him and his animal forebears.

The curriculum emphasizes anthropological, biological, and ethnographic elements (1971) and use of a wide range of media from three categories: films and other visual materials, written materials, and games. Specific materials have been created from ethnographic film studies and field research. They reflect Bruner's notion that human beings translate their experience into a model of the world through actions (the enactive mode), through images (the iconic mode), and through symbols (the symbolic mode).

One of the significant results of field tests of this design was positive changes in teaching style. Teachers become learners—more open and less authoritative—as students become increasingly able to express ideas and share in activities. This holistic approach to curriculum development, changing the behavior of teachers as well as of students, is very desirable and should be encouraged. *Man: A Course of Study* should serve as an excellent "starter model" for further curriculum development in environmental education at the local level.

Brennan and Brandwein (1969) collaborated with South Carolina teachers to develop a series called *People and Their Environment*, also based on an interdisciplinary approach. Three major principles are at the heart of the program: that living things are interdependent with one another and with their environment, that organisms are the products of their heredity and environment, and that organisms and environments constantly change.

SELECTION OF CURRICULUM MATERIALS

The market is rapidly being flooded, or "polluted," with a variety of curriculum materials for environmental studies. The selection and use of these materials by teachers is becoming a crucial problem.

The Committee on Conservation and Environmental Studies of the National Science Teachers Association (1970) has developed criteria for selecting curriculum materials:

1. Materials should include some that provide for the active involvement of individual children and small groups.
2. They should permit open-ended investigation by children, with suggestions for how to pursue these investigations.
3. Materials should provide for firsthand experiences with one or more parts of the child's environment.
4. They should facilitate direct coordination with curricula in science, mathematics, social science, humanities, the arts, health, and physical education.
5. Materials should not only serve to promote environmental "literacy" but should also help to develop an environmental "ethic."
6. Reports of field tests of the materials should be available from the publisher or supplier, as should *provisions for feedback from teachers and readers.*
7. Materials should contain accurate information; they should also be readable, attractive, and free from bias.
8. They should include clearly stated objectives and means for evaluating achievement.
9. The experience and training of the teaching staff should be considered in the selection of curriculum materials.
10. *Materials not expressly designed for special groups should be written so as to be useful for a majority of teachers.*

SPECIFIC ENVIRONMENTAL CURRICULA

The involvement of students in environmental studies may necessitate departures from traditional curricular approaches. Osborn and Spofford (1970) have reported a most intriguing approach to interdisciplinary involvement in environmental field experiences adopted at Jamesville-DeWitt Middle School in Jamesville, New York. Fellows Hill, a New York State reforestation area, is used as an outdoor laboratory for students. Although the main focus is on science, certain activities are arranged to include mathematics, reading, social studies, and English. Once in the outdoor laboratory the students are divided into nine groups with the following assignments:

1. Study of microscopic organisms.
2. Study of bottom-dwelling organisms.

3. Study of larger plants.
4. Study of larger animals.
5. Collection of data on temperature of pond water at various depths.
6. Developing a map representation of the pond's surface including various surface features.
7. Measuring the depth of the pond at several different points.
8. Estimating heights of various plants and trees surrounding the pond.
9. Estimating populations of various pond plants and animals.

Mathematics is used in collection for later class work of data on populations of certain plants and animals and on pond depths and for mapping the pond. English assignments include taking notes and writing poems and imaginative compositions on how living things around the pond might perceive their worlds. Social studies and reading exercises are incorporated in various ways, including a set of "did you know?" questions about the environment.

McGovern (1969) has reported a three-week institute conducted for teachers and students at Tilton School in rural New Hampshire. The major objective was to change attitudes toward environmental problems and to develop curriculum materials for new instructional approaches. The focus was on water pollution. Through involvement in such a "real" problem, participants were able to increase their understanding of its relations to all environmental problems.

After some initial laboratory and field work the students set out to learn how the citizens of Tilton felt about water pollution. This project raised several important issues: "Whom do you ask? What kind of questions? What research techniques do you use?" The results of the survey shocked the students. Only one-fifth of the citizens knew that Tilton had no sewage-treatment facilities. Few people realized that there was any pollution problem at all, even though students' tests of drinking water had revealed it to be impure. This specific curricular approach involved interdisciplinary study and seeking of solutions to an immediate and relevant environmental problem.

Jacobus (1969) has described the efforts of various professionals to develop a curriculum for a school nature site in Lexington, Massachusetts. The development and conservation of such a site can be very useful in an environmental-education program. The first step (after the site was made available to the school) was to determine for what purposes the site would be used. The teachers listed reasons why and how they wanted to use it. Then they became familiar with the site itself and made contacts with other professionals: Expert assistance was provided by the supervisor of conservation education, the local soil-conservation agent, the National Audubon Society representative, and parents who were professionals in related fields.

The curriculum was developed within the following five-part framework: becoming familiar with the site, studying the ecology of the site, soil conservation, introduction to the world of smaller animals, and outdoor winter activities. A matchbox project, a variety of eight-millimeter silent loops, and other materials were integrated with a unit from the Science Curriculum Improvement Study, a model science curriculum developed at the University of California in 1961. The school nature site thus provided an excellent "environmental laboratory" for exploration coordinated with a unit of classroom study. There is great value in permitting children to develop a nature site and thus to cultivate a sense of responsibility and pride.

One of the more effective ways of teaching conservation is based on a year-long cycle of activities. Help in planning such a cycle of activities can be obtained from local agents of state and Federal agricultural and conservation agencies. Shugrue and Ayers (1968) have suggested the calendar of conservation activities shown in Figure 4.2.

An appealing idea has been put forth by Garvey (1969), who has described a nature trail developed for the blind and the partially sighted in the lovely National Arboretum in Washington, D.C. The blind person is guided along the trail by ropes stretched between stations. The stations are points of interest marked with both braille and printed descriptions of the natural phenomena. Points of interest include a rotting tree, a large oak, an open meadow, and plants in a marsh area. The main purpose of the trail is to enable blind people to "observe" the balance of nature.

An investigation of ways to teach outdoor education, conducted by the school districts of North Hempstead, New York, has been reported by Lovett (1969). At the Hampton Street School the teachers designed a program in which a pilot group of eighty-four sixth-grade pupils was taken to summer camp in southern New York state. The planning and preparation for this experience involved parents, teachers, and pupils through the entire nine-month school year. Outdoor education began as soon as the bus left the school. Through the intercom the teachers were able to point out interesting sights. Frequent stops were made to permit the students to investigate natural phenomena. The summer activities occurred both on and off the camp site, and local people were included whenever possible. In the camp there were nature walks, a deerskin trader explained the process of leather tanning, there was a logging demonstration, and a state conservation agent made a presentation. There were also laboratory, language-arts, and art activities; a reenactment of the Olympic Games; family-style meals; group singing, and square dancing. The students left the camp to visit a newspaper publisher, a lumber mill, a dairy farm, a trading post, and a museum village. The entire summer was considered very successful.

PROJECTS	FALL		
	SEPTEMBER	**OCTOBER**	**NOVEMBER**
LAWNS	← Prepare, fertilize soil and seed grass. →		
SOIL	◄ Study the components of soil by examination of samples collected. ◄ Study the processes of soil building through trips into the field.		
FLOWER GROWING	◄ Force bulbs (tulips, white narcissus, hyacinth). Note: Special bulbs for forcing must be purchased. ► Prepare bulb beds (plant tulip, hyacinth, daffodil bulbs). Harvest seeds from previously grown annuals (zinnias, marigolds, cockscomb). Begin composting with leaves, straw, garden and kitchen vegetable refuse. If buried outside, watering not needed.		
VEGETABLE GROWING	◄ Grow lettuce in cold frames. ► ◄		→
WINDOW BOXES			
DISH GARDENS	◄ Prepare any time of year. Plants include: philodendron, cactus, succulents, ivy.		
PROPAGATING ORNAMENTALS Windowsill Greenhouses **Hardwood Cuttings** Layering	◄ Propagate hardwood cuttings—mock orange, lilac, crepe myrtle, forsythia. Bury cuttings below freezing line. →		
TERRARIA			←
TREES	◄ Observe leaves, fruit, bark, root. Press leaves and observe their margins, veins, and midrib. Identify specimens and store for reference. ►		
			◄ Harvest evergreens. Classify as to broad-leaf and needle-leaf varieties. Use cuttings for ornamentation. →

Figure 4.2 A calendar of conservation activities. From Sylvia K. Shugrue and Thomas L. Ayers, "A Concern for Conservation," *Science and Children,* September 1968. Copyright 1968 by the National Science Teachers Association, 1201 Sixteenth St., N.W., Washington, D.C. 20036.

PROJECTS	WINTER		
	DECEMBER	JANUARY	FEBRUARY
LAWNS	The maintenance of the lawn is the responsibility of school ◄ personnel (custodian). To encourage practices of conservation, children can participate in seeding, weeding, and anti-litter campaigns, and identifying native plants. ►		
◄ **SOIL** ──	Study the components of soil by examination of samples collected Study the processes of soil building through trips into the field. ──►		
FLOWER GROWING	Store bulbs potted for forcing for approximately two months ◄ in a cool dark place indoors. Cover with plastic to retain ► water. Add water when necessary. Bulbs buried outside do not require watering.		
		◄──── At two-week intervals, bring stored ─► bulbs into light of classroom, water, and observe flowers develop.	
◄ **VEGETABLE** ── **GROWING**	── Modify soil for growing seedlings and/or vegetables. ──►		
WINDOW BOXES		◄──── Construct window boxes. ────►	
◄ **DISH GARDENS** ──	Prepare any time of year. Plants include: philodendron, cactus, succulents, ivy. ──►		
PROPAGATING ORNAMENTALS Windowsill Greenhouses Hardwood Cuttings Layering		◄─ Propagate conifers such as yew and ─► juniper and broad-leaf evergreens such as pyracanthus, lugustrum, and Chinese holly.	
◄ **TERRARIA** ──	Study the needs of plants. Classify plants according to flowering or nonflowering. Observe the water cycle, the ─► water table, the growth in terraria plants. Ornament the school room or home.		
TREES	Harvest evergreens. Classify as to broad-leaf and needle-leaf varieties. Use cuttings for ─► ornamentation.		
◄	Observe the structure of a tree from the classroom window. ◄ Record changes. Observe trunk, branching, and shape. ►		

SPRING			SUMMER		
MARCH	**APRIL**	**MAY**	**JUNE**	**JULY**	**AUGUST**

◄— Fertilizing, watering, mowing, weed control (custodian). —► | Seed eroded or damaged areas.

◄————— Press and identify native plants. Store samples for reference. —►

◄ Plant flowers and vegetable seeds —► in window boxes or cold frames to be transplanted (February-March).

Plant perenniels outdoors: tiger lilies, daisies, lily-of-the-valley, peonies, pansies. Grow house plants from seed. ►

Plant summer annual flowers: marigolds, petunias, cockscomb, zinnias, nasturtium, asters, morning glories indoors for transplanting after frost.

◄— Seed annuals —— outdoors.

◄— Weed, cultivate, and care for summer flowers. —►

◄ Plan areas and prepare the soil for vegetable gardens. Plant ► vegetables: corn, lettuce, radishes, onion sets, cabbage, mustard greens. Transplant available vegetables and flower seedlings from cold frames.

◄— Weed, cultivate, and harvest vegetables. —►

◄ Prepare the soil and transplant flower seedlings, rooted ► cuttings to pots or window boxes.

◄——— Transplant plants previously propagated into beds. ——►

Propagate garden flowers such as geraniums, lantana, and ◄—flowering shrubs such as forsythia, mock orange, and ► viburnum.

◄— Propagate broad-leaf evergreens —► such as azaleas and camellias.

◄——— Observe the flowering parts of trees. ———► Collect and press leaves of local trees.

Arbor Day

Another approach could focus on involving pupils in improving the quality of the school environment:

1. Constructing color charts and making suggestions for aesthetic improvement of physical facilities.
2. Building aquariums, vivariums, windowsill greenhouses, and terraria to provide in the classroom contacts with the natural world.
3. Helping to keep the facilities and grounds free of pollution.
4. Caring for plants on school grounds.
5. Caring for plants and animals in the school.
6. Making pictures, bulletin boards, models, and other materials to produce a more pleasant atmosphere.
7. Constructing "environmental codes" to guide student behavior.
8. Developing school nature sites.
9. Informing parents of pollution problems in the school.
10. Organizing student task forces to improve environmental quality in the school and larger community.

The United States is not the only nation in which schools are focusing on the environment. Christmas (1970) has reported that ten- and eleven-year-olds from St. Joseph's Roman Catholic School in Deptford, England, spend one day each week at an abandoned school in nearby Kent. In the morning they do their lessons as usual; then they have a picnic lunch, and the fun begins. In Kent the children are surrounded by fresh air, grass, trees, and flowers—a complete change from the asphalt and concrete of their normal environment. They learn to identify trees, shrubs, and small animals. A special feature of the program is that mothers (and sometimes younger siblings) are allowed to go along on the weekly outings. Both children and parents are enthusiastic about the program.

Cretzburg (1970) has described a method of teaching an ecology unit that included a "tutorial" field trip. The first part of the unit was taught inside to give the students enough background to profit from the outdoor experience, which took place in a woodlot. The trail was about a mile long and included forty-two stations. The students were divided into small groups, and each group was given a cassette recorder describing each station. The tape directed students' attention to various points of interest and gave directions for simple experiments that could be performed at each station. The teacher circulated among the groups to assist and to answer questions.

Regardless of the specific curricular approach used, the focus should be upon a conceptual framework of environmental concepts and processes selected from the natural (physical) and social sciences. Emphasis should be on significant concepts and processes, rather than on discrete facts. With clearly specified objectives, teacher and pupils can explore various instructional alternatives for reaching them.

EVALUATING THE ENVIRONMENTAL-EDUCATION PROGRAM

Evaluation should be an integral and continual process, providing the data necessary for improvement of programs. Such programs are effective to the degree that they enable each pupil to acquire ecological concepts and generalizations, practice the skills of critical inquiry, and develop desirable attitudes. Data collected on the following questions, although not totally comprehensive, should assist greatly in evaluation:

1. Does the program draw upon relevant content from the natural (physical) and social sciences?
2. Are the concepts organized in a structure suitable to students' comprehension?
3. Are objectives realistic, comprehensive, and clearly defined? Are they in accord with the students' developmental needs?
4. Are provisions made for student exploration of various components of the biophysical environment? Are appropriate inquiry techniques employed? Are students involved in "real world" problem solving?
5. Are provisions made for student evaluation in the affective, cognitive, and psychomotor domains? Is self-evaluation important?
6. Is the curricular sequence balanced in its progression from kindergarten to twelfth grade?
7. Is there provision for evaluative feedback to improve the program?
8. Are appropriate evaluation instruments and procedures used?
9. Are teaching strategies continually evaluated and improved?
10. Are there criteria for the selection and use of materials?
11. To what degree are teachers involved in curriculum planning and evaluation?
12. Are preservice and in-service programs provided for continual improvement of program personnel?

Measurement is part of the collection of data. Evaluation, a more inclusive concept, involves comparing the data collected to criteria and making judgments. Careful attention should be given to the following tips for evaluation of instruction:

1. State objectives clearly, using behavioral terms.
2. Plan both required and optional activities to fit these objectives.
3. Use a variety of evaluation instruments and procedures.
4. Be sure that any tests used sample what has been taught.
5. Tests should indicate what the teacher values in learning.
6. Promote student self-evaluation.
7. Continue teacher self-evaluation.
8. Use data thus gathered to improve the quality of instruction.

We collect volumes of data, but too often they are "dead data." To be effective, we must use them to improve programs. Furthermore, the quality of the data collected is directly correlated with the quality of the assessment tools and procedures used. Careful and continuous attention to these factors should result in a better program.

SUMMARY

The development and implementation of environmental education curricula are among the most urgent needs of the 1970s. The Environmental Education Act is designed to provide funds for this purpose throughout the nation. The environmental education curriculum should begin in the elementary school with emphasis upon developing a citizen who understands the biophysical environment and problems related to it, understands how to help solve this problem, and is motivated toward positive action to achieve these ends.

An interdisciplinary design that incorporates exploration of the physical, social, and man-made environments is most desirable. The teacher should be encouraged to use a variety of instructional approaches designed to involve pupils in meaningful experiences. Care should be employed in the selection and utilization of environmental education materials. Each curriculum should be continuously evaluated to insure quality.

The development of an effective environmental education curriculum is a challenge that requires our expertise. It could well be the key to survival in the last quarter of this century.

INVESTIGATIONS

1. Conduct a survey to ascertain what state and local committees are engaged in developing curricula and programs for environmental education. To what degree are these various groups working together? What recommendations can you make?

2. Carefully examine all the materials of *Man: A Course of Study*, a flexible program for upper elementary- and middle-school children (Bruner,

1965). Review the various evaluation reports of the pilot testing in various school divisions. If possible, visit a school district that is currently using this program. Share your findings with the class.

3. What are the major features of *People and Their Environment* (Brennan & Brandwein, 1969). Prepare a comparative analysis of this curriculum and of *Man: A Course of Study* (Bruner, 1965).

4. A special report by the editors of Education U.S.A. (1971) concluded that environmental education is crucial but that few students are exposed to it. The report also concluded that some of the existing programs are good but that most fall seriously short. Examine this report carefully, and discuss in class its implications for curriculum development.

5. Visit a local elementary school and collect data on pupil population, curriculum, staff, facilities, and community. Based upon this research, develop a general plan for an environmental-education curriculum in that school. Present your plan to the school faculty, and discuss its strengths and weaknesses. Suggest that the faculty use it as a springboard for developing its own curriculum.

6. Develop a framework for evaluating an existing environmental-education curriculum, with specific attention to objectives, content, required and optional experiences, evaluative procedures, materials, interdisciplinary characteristics, and related components.

7. Plan and conduct in class a panel discussion with an ecologist, an industrialist, a parent, a student, and an elementary-school teacher, focusing on the topic "What the elementary school child should know about his environment."

8. Prepare a plan for a workshop for elementary-school teachers focusing on the question "What should the classroom teacher know about environmental education?"

REFERENCES

Baker, Paul T. "The Application of Ecological Theory to Anthropology," *American Anthropologist*, 64:15–22, 1962.

Brennan, Matthew J. & Paul F. Brandwein (eds.). *People and Their Environment: Teachers Curriculum Guide to Conservation Education.* 8 vols. Chicago: Ferguson, 1969.

Bruner, Jerome. *Man: A Course of Study. Social Studies Curriculum Program Occasional Paper*, No. 3. Cambridge, Mass.: Educational Services, 1965.

Carter, Luther J. "Environmental Studies: OST Report Urges Better Effort," *Science*, 166:851, November 14, 1969.

Christmas, Linda. "Breakout to Green Fields," *The New York Times Educational Supplement*, 3863, April 3, 1970.

"Committee on Conservation and Environmental Studies of The National Science Teachers Association," *Science Teacher*, 37:35, May 1970.

"Congress: USOE Plan Aid for Environmental Education," *Phi Delta Kappan*, 51:569, June 1970.

Congressional Record. 91st Congress, 116:H187, Part 1, Washington, D.C., 1970.

Cretzburg, Earl R. "Audio-Tutorial Field Trip," *The American Biology Teacher*, 32:301, May 1970.

Curriculum Development Associates. *Man: A Course of Study*. Washington, D.C., 1971.

Edgerton, Robert B. " 'Cultural' vs. 'Ecological' Factors in the Expression of Values, Attitudes, and Personality Characteristics," *American Anthropologist*, 67:442–447, April 1965.

Education U.S.A. (ed.). *Environment and the Schools: Pioneer Programs Set the Pace for States and Districts*, Washington, D.C.: Author, 1971.

Fischer, John. "Survival U: Prospectus for a Really Relevant University," *Harper's*, 239:12–22, September 1969.

Garvey, Joseph. "Touch and See Nature Trail," *Science and Children*, October 1969.

Hare, F. Kenneth. "How Should We Treat Environment?" *Science*, 167:352–355, January 1970.

Hill, Wilhelmina. "Environmental Education: The State of the Art," *Childhood Education*, 47:14–18, October 1970.

Jacobus, John E. "A Team Effort to Develop a Curriculum for a School Nature Site," *Science Education*, December 1969.

Karplus, Robert & Herbert D. Thier. *A New Look at Elementary School Science*. Chicago: Rand McNally, 1967.

Lovett, Thomas B. "Outdoor Education at Camp," *Science and Children*, May 1969.

McGovern, Alan. "Getting Their Feet Wet," *Environment*, 11:25–27, November 1969.

Osborn, Ron & Roger Spofford. "Interdisciplinary Involvement in Environmental Field Trips," *Science Teacher*, 37:73–74, April 1970.

Sale, Larry L. "Environmental Education in the Elementary School," *North Carolina Education*, 1:12–13, 30–31, October 1970.

Shugrue, Sylvia K. & Thomas L. Ayers. "A Concern for Conservation," *Science and Children*, September 1968.

Stapp, William B. *Integrating Conservation and Outdoor Education into the Curriculum (K–12)*. Minneapolis: Burgess, 1965.

Task Force on Environmental Health and Related Problems, U.S. Department of Health, Education, and Welfare. *A Strategy for a Livable Environment*. Washington, D.C.: Government Printing Office, 1967.

part two / *areas of instruction*

chapter 5 / pollution of the environment

There was a time when people believed that any man was entitled to all the fresh air and water that he needed to live in good health. Many of us can also remember when there was plenty of virgin soil for a person willing to move to a new frontier. Most of us have never felt concern about having enough fuel to heat our houses, drive our automobiles, and operate our electrical appliances, provided that we have had means to pay for these needs. Now, in the 1970s, we find ourselves bombarded with reports with dire implications for the future survival of mankind unless drastic action is taken to stop the pollution of our air, water, and soil and the depletion of our natural resources.

"Environmental quality," a term introduced by the National Wildlife Federation, refers to the conditions that make life possible or tolerable—or the contrary ("Our National Environmental Quotient," 1969). Solid-waste disposal, contamination of the atmosphere through the proposed supersonic transport, stepped-up eutrophication of bodies of water, over-crowding of people in urban areas, damage to animal life through DDT and other residual insecticides and herbicides, destruction of animal and plant life through oil spillage, sound pollution, and thermal pollution are only a few of the environmental concerns that are presently being debated far and wide.

Pollutants are largely products of physical and biological forces that are constantly operating on the earth. Animals produce carbon dioxide, volcanoes emit sulfur dioxide, and movements of the wind constantly swirl solid particles into the air. The normal forces of erosion create a great many kinds of particles in both air and water as they move through cycles of constant change. Animals produce solid waste products that are returned to air, soil, and water and decomposed into new elements or compounds that can be used by other animals or plants. These same natural products become pollutants when excessively concentrated so that unhealthy or unlivable conditions for plants and animals, including man, are the result.

Heightened concern over these various types of pollution in the late 1960s probably arose largely from recognition that man has run out of space where he can move when he feels too crowded or when conditions become too unpleasant for him. Scientific and technological advances have produced changes in transportation and communications that make it possible for a person to talk to anyone on earth in a matter of minutes and to travel to almost any part of the earth in a day. These advances have included many types of combustion processes in industry, power plants, and automobiles, which have released vast quantities of pollutants into the earth's atmosphere.

AIR POLLUTION

Any investigation of pollution should begin with the air and its contaminants. Good air is so essential to human survival that a few minutes' deprivation can result in irreparable damage to the central nervous system. Today we know of many disease germs that are carried by air. Everyone has experienced the discomfort of breathing air containing too much smoke or a high ratio of dust particles. Many people suffer the chronic discomforts of hay fever and other allergies stimulated by contents of the air breathed.

By far the greatest source of air pollution is the internal-combustion engine. The 109 million motor vehicles in the United States are nearly all powered by such engines, which burn gasoline. This type of engine is efficient in its ability to convert fuel to energy to propel a large vehicle, but one of its important by-products is carbon monoxide. Automobiles in the United States emit more than 66 million tons of carbon monoxide annually. Other contaminants of air released by motor vehicles include hydrocarbons, at the rate of 12 million tons a year, and nitrogen oxides, at the rate of 6 million tons. Automobiles also emit at least 1 ton of sulfur oxides and 1 ton of particulate matter each year. These figures total to 86 million tons of air pollutants from motor vehicles alone ("Sources of Air Pollution and Their Control," 1968).

The second most prominent source of air pollution is industry, which releases 23 million tons of pollutants annually, the chief ones being sulfur oxides (9 million tons), which are by-products of the burning of coal, particularly soft coal. Power plants, space heating, and refuse disposal are the other principal sources of air pollution, with sulfur oxides, nitrogen oxides, carbon monoxide, hydrocarbons, and particulate matter as the pollutants.

Air pollution is one of the most dangerous forms of pollution, for we all need air to live; sulfur oxides, nitrogen oxides, carbon monoxide, and hydrocarbons are essentially invisible to us, but they can nevertheless be lethal. Each person needs an average of thirty pounds of air a day in order to remain alive. Already there are reports of children's health having been permanently altered by pollution of the air that they breathe. Air pollution that causes gradual damage to the human body receives little notice. Sudden and serious pollution that causes many rapid deaths brings cries of alarm for immediate remedial action. Unfortunately, even when such disasters have occurred in some areas, no immediate corrective measures have been possible. The industrialized, motorized sources of pollution cannot be drastically reduced until people accept an entirely different living style.

Smog

Smog is a combination of "smoke" and "fog." A slow, killing smog usually includes an unusually severe temperature inversion. Under normal conditions warmer air rises, and its molecules spread farther apart, which cools it. In a temperature inversion the upper air is already hotter than the ground air and thus prevents the normal rise of warm air. The trapped ground air becomes progressively more foul as the temperature inversion continues (McDermott, 1961).

Perhaps the most familiar example of a smog that caused a large number of deaths (more than 4,000) occurred on December 5–9, 1952, in London. It became a major killer because high concentrations of sulfur dioxide from soft-coal fires used to heat homes built up in the ground air. Since 1958, when the Clean Air Act was passed, there has been steady improvement in the London air. Once considered one of the dirtiest and unhealthiest cities in the world, London now rates far above New York City, Tokyo, Los Angeles, and other comparable cities. This change is a notable example of how some governments have reacted to pollution problems, one that those who find polluted conditions in the United States today almost hopeless might take as a model.

On October 26, 1948, Donora, Pennsylvania, suffered a severe pollution catastrophe in which twenty people died and 43 percent of the population became ill. A steel factory, a sulfuric-acid plant, and a zinc plant were all releasing fumes into the atmosphere, which was hit by a temperature inversion and fog. The general opinion is that the sulfuric fumes were present in normal amounts but that the temperature inversion and fog made them deadly.

Carbon Monoxide

When the American housewife lights the charcoal grill in her backyard or the gas range in her kitchen, when the blast furnace roars away at a steel mill, or when any of us starts an automobile, the atmosphere receives carbon monoxide (CO) in quantities unknown before these appliances were developed. Carbon monoxide results from fire, and man's discovery of the many uses to which it can be put has greatly increased the amounts of it deposited in our air.

Carbon monoxide is a colorless, odorless gas, a product of incomplete combustion. The mechanism by which a person dies from breathing it is suffocation. Hemoglobin, the molecules of blood that contain iron, picks up oxygen in the lungs, forming a loose complex. This oxygen is then delivered through the arteries to the brain, liver, and all other vital organs and tissues of the body, after which the paler colored blood returns by the veins to the lungs for a new supply of oxygen. Hemoglobin has an affinity for carbon monoxide, so that, if the latter is present in the lungs, even in fairly small amounts, the hemoglobin will absorb it before oxygen. The affinity of hemoglobin for carbon monoxide is more than 200 times greater than that for oxygen. The carbon monoxide thus robs the blood of its oxygen supply, and the brain and other organs and tissues begin to starve. The brain cannot be deprived of oxygen for more than about eight minutes without permanent damage (Carr, 1965).

The internal-combustion engine, which powers by far the majority of motor vehicles in this country, is the primary culprit in carbon-monoxide poisoning. It is efficient, economical, and fast-working, but the price of these advantages is incomplete combustion of fuel. The compound of hydrogen and carbon, called a hydrocarbon, used to fuel a gasoline engine unites with oxygen to produce carbon dioxide, water, and energy. If the carburetor is adjusted to a rich air-fuel mixture, containing more fuel than can be completely burned to carbon dioxide and water, then additional power is available for rapid acceleration. And more carbon monoxide is released into the atmosphere. It has been estimated that 1,000 automobiles will release about 3 tons of carbon monoxide into the air each day. There were 109 million motor vehicles in operation in the United States in 1970, an increase of 4 million over the preceding year.

WATER POLLUTION

Except for the air that we breathe, water is probably the environmental factor most important to human survival. One adult human being requires about 2,500 gallons of water a day for his maintenance, including water actually consumed and that needed to grow his food. In the United States our present water consumption exceeds 15,000 gallons per person per day;

we use it to produce clothing, to flush toilets, to manufacture goods, and to air-condition our homes, offices, and other buildings, as well as numerous other personal uses.

The enormous amount of water required to grow a plant, which is multiplied many times to grow an animal, should impress on us all our utter dependence upon water. It is estimated that around 1,000 pounds of water are used to produce 1 pound of milling wheat, or 1 pound of bread. A gallon of water weighs 8.3 pounds; 300 gallons are therefore required to make 2½ pounds of wheat flour.

To grow 25 pounds of alfalfa more than 2,300 gallons of water are required. This amount of hay produces approximately 1 pound of meat on a beef cow. If we imagine a generous American diet of 1 pound of animal fat and protein and 2 pounds of vegetable foods per day, then 2,300 gallons of water to produce the animal portion and around 200 gallons to produce the vegetable portion would be required (Nikolaieff, 1967).

More important than these quantities is man's utter dependence upon water for survival, even for a short time. We take water for granted, but a person can survive only about three days without it.

Water seldom stands still in nature. Yielding to the laws of gravity, it flows across the earth's surface in streams to lakes, ponds, and estuaries and ultimately to the oceans. It is evaporated from these bodies by solar energy and is transported over great distances in the atmosphere. Natural processes of evaporation, gravitational flow, and transpiration from plants create an endless, dynamic hydrologic cycle, one that includes unlimited opportunities for pollution.

Polluted water is water that contains substances harmful to man or to some of the plant and wildlife upon which man depends. Almost all pollutants of water (various bacteria, minerals, organic chemicals, sewage, solid wastes, and metals) are beneficial to mankind in some circumstances, but in large quantities they can be harmful to man's health and well being.

Major Sources

Sewage and other fluid wastes are poured into the nation's waterways at a rate of 2 million gallons a second. This pollution comes primarily from three sources: industry, agriculture, and municipalities. The drinking-water supplies in many American cities are being threatened. Eighty-four major cities have been reported as having substandard water systems—that is, they failed to meet all the standards for both facilities and water quality set by the U.S. Public Health Service (Lindsay, 1970).

Residual pesticides—those that do not undergo chemical decomposition in nature—are being more and more recognized as severe threats to fish, birds, and other wildlife. The principal category of such residuals includes chlorinated hydrocarbons like DDT and dieldrin, aldrin, heptachlor, lindane, chlordane, and endrin. These compounds are practically insoluble in water and resist decomposition in the natural environment.

Pesticide residues are responsible for an unusually DDT concentration in fish caught in Santa Monica Bay, near Los Angeles. Some fish have had as many as thirty parts of DDT per million parts of body weight. Federal standards prohibit sale of fish with DDT concentrations higher than five parts per million. Sewage emptied into the bay has been blamed as the principal culprit.

Carson brought to public attention the danger of continued use of such pesticides to birds and fish in *Silent Spring* in 1962. A more detailed examination of the effects of DDT on human food supplies and thus on human health will be conducted in Chapter 6.

Since Carson's book was published, manufacturers of pesticides have attempted to belittle the importance of her message, but evidence supporting it has continued to mount; nevertheless, both government and industry have continued to use persistent pesticides. In *Since Silent Spring* (1970), Frank Graham, Jr., has further documented Carson's argument.

The Federal government has banned the use of persistent insecticides on Federal lands, and the three companies responsible for manufacturing more than 50 percent of the DDT produced in this country—Olin Corporation, Allied Chemical, and Diamond Shamrock Corporation—have recently announced plans to discontinue its production.

Contamination of a Body of Water

Household detergents are one group of pollutants that have contributed to rapid contamination of Lake Erie. Detergents contain phosphates, which contribute to rapid growth of algae in bodies of water, resulting in overcrowding and death through insufficiency of sunlight. Bacteria then proliferate to feed on the dead algae, helping to deplete the oxygen supply so that they too suffocate and die. Of course, any other contaminant that rapidly reduces the oxygen supply in a river or lake can kill massive numbers of fish. After a heavy rainstorm, fish deaths resulting from floods of raw sewage into rivers have been reported. Raw sewage must have an abundance of oxygen present in order to undergo the decay process by which it is returned to the water and to the land in a natural state. There simply is not enough oxygen both to oxidize the sewage and to maintain fish life.

Oil Spills

Twelve oil wells being brought into production by the Chevron Oil Company in the Gulf of Mexico southeast of New Orleans caught fire in February 1970. When the fires were extinguished, oil continued to gush into the gulf waters for three weeks, producing a massive slick that drifted toward waters containing redhead ducks and into the oyster beds along the Louisiana coast. Major biological damage was prevented by unseasonable northerly winds that kept the oil at sea, although long-term results are less clear-cut.

In February 1969 a giant oil slick had spread through the Santa Barbara channel on the coast of California. Beaches, harbors, and nearly all reaches of the 1,800-square-mile channel were covered with the oil, which had spilled from a "blown" oil well as a result of offshore drilling by the Union Oil Company. Certainly the most immediate victims of this tragedy were the birds washed up on the beaches: western grebes, sandpipers, plovers, surf skaters, and several species of ducks. These birds attempted to clean their wings and thus swallowed the toxic oil. A dolphin, its breathing holes choked with oil, was washed up on the beach dead. Some nineteen or more solutions were attempted before the oil flow was stopped. Even then it was estimated that three to five years would be necessary to restore the sands. Over a five-month period 3 million gallons of oil had poured into the channel.

The *Torrey Canyon*, a superfreighter, broke up off the Cornish coast of England in April 1967, spilling 36 million gallons of oil into the English Channel and causing a similar disaster to beaches, birds, and other life along the south coast of England. Every living thing in the path of the ugly globs of reeking sludge was smothered or poisoned as the oil moved from the wrecked ship toward the coasts of Cornwall. Efforts to break up, destroy, divert, or dissolve the crude-oil slick were unsuccessful.

Cleaning the oil from the feathers of birds unfortunately also destroys their natural protective oils, and it may take months for a bird to molt and grow new feathers.

Calefaction

"Calefaction" is a term for warming of river, lake, and estuary waters by electric-power and other industries; it endangers fish and other creatures living in these waters. Fish, which are cold-blooded animals, are particularly sensitive to thermal changes in their environment. The impact of temperature on their rate of metabolism is most notable: "Generally speaking the metabolic rate doubles with each increase of 10 degrees Celcius (18 degrees F.)" (Clark, 1969). Such an acceleration increases the need for oxygen, and the animal's respiration rate also rises.

Electric-power generators are the principal sources of heat released into bodies of water. Hot water is drained into these bodies after it has been used to cool the steam condensers. The construction of large generating plants fueled by nuclear energy means much greater thermal pollution. Nuclear fuel wastes 60 percent more energy than does fossil fuel, and that energy is released as heat in the water used to cool the condensers. In 1970 there were seventeen nuclear-powered electric generating plants in operation in the United States; forty-nine more were under construction, and forty-four were in the active planning stages. They also raise the possibility of hazardous radiation.

Merriman (1970) has reported a detailed long-range study of the Connecticut River, which flows about 400 miles along the boundary of Vermont and New Hampshire, through Massachusetts and Connecticut, and into Long Island Sound. Six power plants use water from this river for cooling. Since the study was begun in 1965 no drastic biological consequences have been found attributable to the warming of its waters, however.

Metal Pollutants

Several metallic by-products of industrial processes are toxic to fish and other life in lakes and streams. In the 1950s mercury poisoning was responsible for killing or disabling 111 people who ate fish contaminated with this element from a plastics plant in Japan. Mercury compounds were suspected of causing three members of a New Mexico family to be grotesquely disabled after eating meat from pigs that had been fed grain treated with fungicides.

Metallic mercury is used in electrode pairs to produce sodium hydroxide and chlorine gas when electric current is passed through solutions of sodium chloride. This mercury has apparently leaked into the effluence emptied into the Detroit River and Lake Erie.

SOIL POLLUTION

Soil pollutants are essentially the same substances that pollute water and air: deposited chemicals and solid wastes. Inadequately treated sewage, synthetic detergents, wastes from cattle feed lots, inorganic fertilizers, and insecticides and herbicides all tend to disrupt the natural biological cycles involving soil and water. Nitrogen oxides released into the air by internal-combustion engines are readily converted by sunlight into nitrates and then deposited in the soil and surface water by rain and snow.

Solid-waste pollutants, junked automobiles, tin cans, glass bottles, and paper and plastic products add to the debris that is devastating the beauty of our countryside and damaging the soil necessary to human well-being.

Pesticides and Herbicides

If one square meter of soil were carefully examined and screened for all its living matter, it might contain as many as 1 million arthropods and even more nematodes and protozoans. The "biomass," or weight, of all the soil animals (exclusive of microorganisms) in such an area can total as much as 500 grams, or approximately 1 pound (Edwards, 1969). Earthworms are the most frequent inhabitants of the surface soil; the earthworm population in an average acre of pasture may weigh 500 kilograms, as much as a steer. The majority of soil animals are found within three inches of the ground surface; their importance cannot be overemphasized. They are responsible for breaking down plant residues and working them into the soil, and their burrowing creates conditions—air spaces and friability—that encourage plant growth.

Large quantities of pesticides, herbicides, and fumigants used on crops and woodlands are the most important threats to the animals in the upper layer of the soil. The more persistent insecticides, like DDT and other chlorinated hydrocarbons, have the most drastic impact. Fumigants are injected directly into the soil in the gaseous state and kill almost everything in the treated area. As they generally do not persist, however, the soil can be fairly quickly repopulated. Herbicides have limited direct effects; Edwards (1969) found that their use does not constitute a serious hazard to the soil community.

Solid Waste

Approximately 4 million automobiles are scrapped each year in the United States, adding vast new tracts of ugliness to the landscape. The Federal government has estimated that about 360 million tons of household, commercial, and industrial waste are generated annually, including 48 billion metal cans, 26 billion glass bottles, and 65 billion metal caps and plastic crowns.

A ton of empty cans, bottles, paper packages, corrugated boxes, and plastic containers is disposed of by the average family in the United States each year: a vast monument to the nature of twentieth-century living that overflows our countryside and garbage-disposal areas. Paper products can be burned, though air pollution from burning necessitates a new approach to incineration. Metal and plastics corrode slowly; most are not biodegradable: They will not decompose by biological action when deposited on the land.

Some methods for disposing of solid waste are being developed. Shredders reduce junked automobiles to a form that can be reprocessed in the steel mills. A Japanese firm has developed a process by which raw garbage can be compressed into blocks under 3,000 pounds of pressure per square inch. The resulting blocks are sufficiently dense and sterile to be used in construction or dumped into the sea.

Chrome- and resin-coated steel cans are replacing tin cans, because they can be more easily recycled. Aluminum cans are being reclaimed by some companies for recycling.

Surface Mining

Figures released by the U.S. Department of the Interior on January 1, 1965, revealed that 3.2 million acres of land in the United States had been disturbed by surface mining (McCullough, 1969). Strip mining for coal, primarily in Kentucky, Pennsylvania, Ohio, and West Virginia, has been the largest single source of this kind of devastation. Bulldozers and mining machinery used in open-pit copper, iron, and aluminum mines also devastate the landscape. Past practices included removing topsoil, rocks, and clay by simply shoving them down the mountainside—with them went the trees and all the other vegetation necessary to preserve soil. Then the exposed coal- or metal-bearing ore was removed, leaving a vast gaping hole that was in many instances unable to support any form of plant life. "Spoil banks," as accumulations of earth and mangled trees are called, are unstable because of effects of gravity and rainfall. Often farmland and homes in the path of a spoil bank are submerged under silt, gravel, and all the debris of the mining operation.

Not only is land destroyed by mining operations, but also exposed mines often release poisonous sulfuric acid or mineral salts onto the surrounding land, killing vegetation and preventing future growth.

SOUND POLLUTION

Noise has joined unclean air, dirty water, and polluted soil as a fourth major threat to the environment. It consists of intrusive and unwanted sounds above a certain tolerance level. Sounds are produced by small local fluctuations in atmospheric pressure that impinge upon the eardrum. Sound vibrations can be transmitted through solids, liquids, and gases.

To understand how sound is produced and transmitted, we can consider a guitar string. When it is plucked it sets in motion waves that successively compress and expand the surrounding air. Sound is thus transmitted through compressible matter: air. It travels at 1,130 feet a second in air, 4,500 feet a second in water, and 15,000 feet a second in steel. It thus travels more rapidly in denser media.

Units called "decibels" measure the energy actually exerted against the eardrum. Table 5.1 gives the decibels for some common sound sources.

How Sound Affects People

In a 1968 report the Federal Council for Science and Technology noted that at least 6 million (and perhaps 16 million) Americans were working under conditions that might impair their hearing (*Noise—Sound Without Value*, 1968). People in all walks of life are subjected to excessive noise. Cities seem to be at the pinnacle of noise pollution, for roaring motor

Table 5.1. Sound-Pressure Levels

Source	Decibels
Jet plane at 100 feet	140
Threshold of pain	130
Riveter	120
Threshold of discomfort	120
Rock-and-roll music	120
Textile loom	107
City traffic	90–110
Vacuum cleaner	70
Conversation	60
Soft whisper	30
Leaves rustling in a breeze	20
Threshold of hearing	0

vehicles, clattering garbage cans, blaring horns, and grinding construction work seem to be constants in city life. People who live near airports are constantly bombarded by the roar of jet aircraft taking off and landing.

Physiological effects of noise exposure below the threshold of pain usually include headaches and temporary loss of hearing. Gradual permanent impairment may develop from continued exposure. Constriction of blood vessels, skin pallor, and dilation of the pupils can be caused by extremely loud noise, whereas certain noises produce changes in basal metabolism, respiration, circulation, and muscle tension. Some workers exposed to noise over long periods have complained of chronic gastritis, nausea, and vomiting. Breysse (1970) has reported a sound-pressure level of 122 decibels at one rock-and-roll dance. He has also described an experiment in which a Florida physician tested the hearing of ten teenagers before a dance and again immediately after the dance. All had suffered significant temporary hearing impairment. Although this observation alone does not lead to general conclusions about damage to young people from the noises they encounter, it definitely warns of possible danger.

Sonic Boom

An aircraft flying more rapidly than the speed of sound creates a pressure wave similar to the bow wave of a boat moving through water. This pressure wave spreads behind the airplane in the shape of a cone. When the cone meets the ground, it can be reflected, thus reinforcing the pressure. People hear the familiar "sonic boom" when the pressure cone sweeps past them on the ground. It is a different phenomenon from the noise produced by an aircraft engine. The effects of sonic booms are still largely unknown. If a supersonic transport is developed and put into commercial use, we may anticipate that the sonic boom will become as much part of our environment as is the noise of aircraft today.

INVESTIGATIONS

Air Pollution

1. Observe a snowfall after several days. Where does the gray color come from?

2. Hold a cold saucer close to the flame of a lighted candle. What do you see forming on the saucer? What happens in the air when the candle is blown out?

3. Notice the back of a bus above the exhaust pipe. What do you see? Watch a car that is emitting black smoke from its exhaust pipe. What is probably wrong with its engine?

4. Press a quart (or larger) milk bottle to your lips and blow hard, to build up pressure in the jar. Suddenly release your mouth. What happens? Now put a smoldering piece of cloth or a wick into the jar, and again blow to build up pressure and release. What happens in the jar? What conditions similar to the atmospheric conditions that produce smog were present? (Warm air saturated with moisture and dust particles is cooled against the surface of the container, causing condensation. In smog warm ground air is trapped below warmer air in the presence of particulate matter produced from burning processes.)

5. Following the instructions on the seed packet, plant several white-petunia seeds in each of six pots containing potting soil or peat moss. After the seedlings are about two inches tall examine the effects of at least two kinds of air pollution on them. Use two plants as controls; then expose two plants to the fumes from burning matches and two plants to the fumes from a burning cigarette lighter. To produce the two types of pollutants needed for this investigation, place wide-mouthed quart jars over the plant pots. Fill two jars with fumes from two or three burning wooden matches. Let the matches burn while the jars are inverted over them for about a minute. Then tighten a lid on the jars until you are ready to invert them over the petunia plants. Follow a similar procedure to collect two jars of gas from a burning cigarette lighter. When you have collected the four jars of pollutants, making sure that all jars are labeled, place them over the four experimental petunia plants. Place empty jars over

the control plants. Leave for fifteen minutes. Repeat this procedure once a week, making sure not to contaminate the control plants. Keep accurate records of your observations of these plants. What differences do you observe in the heights, sizes, colors, and vitality of the plants? What pollutants could you use for other investigations of air pollution on plants? *Caution*: Many common air pollutants, including sulfur oxides, nitrogen oxides, and carbon monoxide, are poisonous and should not be handled by inexperienced people.

6. Look at a ray of sunlight to see if dust particles are present. Or darken a room, and turn on a flashlight or slide projector to search for such particles. Exactly what do you see?

7. Spread a thin coat of petroleum jelly on a clean glass plate or slide plate, and attach the plate to a clothes line with a clothespin. Place several such plates in different locations around a neighborhood where children live. After twenty-four hours bring the slides to school and examine them under a microscope. Record the location and length of exposure for each slide. What relations can be established between the proportion of air pollutants present and the locations of collecting stations; are there industrial sites, incinerators, highways, and so on, near the stations?

8. Bring to school mold from bread or spoiled citrus fruit. Look at the spores under a microscope. Do you think spores from fungi can be carried by air?

9. To learn how an electrostatic precipitator in a smokestack might work, place on a piece of paper piles of dust collected in the room, soot collected from a cold surface held against a candle flame, fine soil, and iron filings. With a hard-rubber comb, comb your hair rapidly; then try to pick up particles from each of these piles. What particles might be attracted to an electrostatic precipitator?

10. Prepare an apparatus to demonstrate how a thermal inversion can generate smog in a heavily populated area. Construct a box like that in Figure 5.1, with a glass front and a glass or clear-polyethylene panel in back, so that children can look inside. With a 100-watt light bulb heat the upper compartment while introducing smoke by means of a smoldering rag or wick inserted through the side hole and then removed when the compartment is full of smoke. The hole should then be plugged. The compartments must be airtight, so that the smoke and hot air remain in them. Now slide out the middle partition. The smoke-filled air should be held down by the hot air in the upper compartment, as in a thermal inversion.

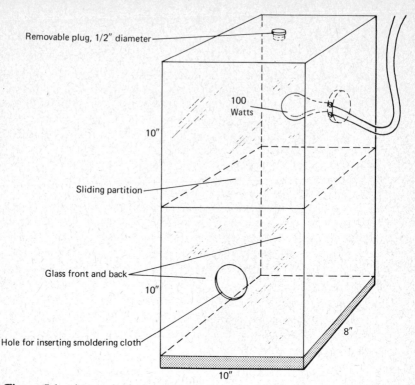

Figure 5.1 Atmospheric inversion box.

11. If sulfur is available, place a small amount (10 grams) on an asbestos pad and light it with a match to demonstrate the acrid, suffocating odor. As a fume-exhaust hood will probably not be available, this exercise should be done outdoors and *only by the teacher*. Children should not inhale quantities of this gas.

Water Pollution

1. Children should be given the opportunity to observe a jar of clean water contrasted with one containing mud. A quart jar is large enough for an impressive contrast. Shake up the muddy water, and leave it standing overnight. The next day should bring questions and investigations of how impurities can be removed from water.

Prepare a filter system by using a one-gallon plastic bottle, cutting off the bottom, and inverting it so that the mouth can be placed in a quart jar, which will catch the filtered water. Put in a piece of large gravel that cannot pass through the mouth. Then add 2-inch layers of smaller gravel, coarse sand, and fine sand in that order. Pour muddy water into the filter. What pollutants are removed? Does the filtered water look clean? Dissolve food coloring or copper sulfate in a quart of water. What happens when this solution is passed through the filter? Do the gravel and sand filter out the dissolved matter? Have children collect samples of water from several sources in the school neighborhood. Look at those containing organic matter, and examine some of the pollutants. Caution must be exercised with water taken from unsanitary sources. Children should be cautioned not to drink any water unless it is known to be sanitary for drinking purposes. They should also wash themselves thoroughly after collecting samples from possibly contaminated streams or ponds.

2. Prepare a simple distillation device, using a teakettle that can be heated on a hot plate. Connect a rubber tube to the spout, and run the other end into a pint jar; seal the joints with modeling clay. Set the jar in a larger container of ice.

   Try distilling water that has not been filtered. Does it appear clean? Next try distilling water containing dissolved coloring matter. Is the distilled water clear?

3. Try washing dirty hands without soap. Then use soap. What difference do you observe? What effect does adding soap have on the cleansing action of water? Collect samples of water from a fast-moving stream, a slow-moving stream, and a pond of standing water. Let a quart of each of these samples stand overnight. The next day measure the height of the sediment in each jar with a meter stick.

4. Obtain samples of water from the school water supply, rain water caught in a plastic pail (or melting snow), and distilled water. Add a measured amount of detergent to a pint of water from each of these three samples. Are there any differences in the amounts of suds? (If the local water is not hard, Epsom salts added to water will "harden" it for testing purposes.) Repeat these tests with soap powder.

5. Use two gallon pickle or mayonnaise jars that have been thoroughly cleaned. In jar A put fresh water from a stream or lake that has stood in the room for at least twenty-four hours. In jar B use similar water that has been boiled for thirty minutes (to evaporate the oxygen) and then cooled to room temperature. Put two fish in each jar. Keep a record of when the fish are added and when any of them dies. In which jar do the fish live longer? Why?

6. Prepare jars C and D with fresh natural water. Add two fish to each. Add ten cubic centimeters of vinegar to jar C. Keep a chronicle of

changes. What conclusions can be drawn about the chemically polluted water?

7. Prepare jars E and F with fresh natural water, and add two fish to each. Record the temperature of each. Now rapidly add hot water to jar E. What do you observe about effects of sudden temperature change on fish life?

8. Place a chicken or other bird feather in a beaker of water. Rub grease or oil on another feather, and place it in the water. What difference do you note in the behavior of the two feathers?

   Put a small amount of oil (used oil from a service station will impress the color and consistency upon children) in a flat pan of water. Notice how the water and oil react to each other. Take a feather and stir the water. What do you notice? How do you think a bird might be able to move after being in water containing spilled oil?

Soil Pollution

1. To determine the most desirable soil conditions for plant growth involves a long-range study, extending perhaps an entire semester. Obtain samples of soil from various locations, including topsoil from a pupil's yard; subsoil of a different color, texture, and composition; clay soil from a stream bank, rich humus from under the layers of fresh leaves and organic matter in the woods; and sandy soil. Examine these samples closely, comparing their structure, color, texture, and friability.

   Using simple test kits (which are commercially available), test pH in each of these soils. Hydrion paper, chemically treated paper that changes color according to the acidity or alkalinity of the tested substance is useful. A color-comparison chart makes approximation of the pH possible. Children in fifth or sixth grade can become aware of pH as a scale for measuring the acidity or alkalinity of a substance.

   Carefully study soil from each sample, using a magnifying glass. Locate any living organisms that are present. Use a microscope to examine a drop of water taken from a jar containing some soil from each sample. How many organisms can be identified?

   Growing plants in these soil samples takes both time and patience. Set up controlled investigations to determine whether or not seeds will germinate in each. Use quick-germinating seeds like corn, beans, and radishes. Temperature and moisture conditions must be controlled in each test pot. Records of planting, watering, and temperature must be kept. Allow students to think up their own investigations of plant growth and to carry them out.

After determining which soils germinate and grow plants best, investigate the effects of soil pollutants on plant growth. Various pollutants can be investigated, but appropriate precautions should be taken if volatile or poisonous substances are used. Kerosene, burnt motor oil, water in which household detergents have been mixed, insect sprays, concentrated fertilizers, and water from polluted ponds are some pollutants to be investigated.

2. Animal life in soils should also be investigated. Use soil samples containing earthworms to find which soil environments are most conducive to growth. Identify any insects found in your soil samples, and observe whether or not they continue to live when various pollutants are added. Investigate the extent to which soil organisms continue to grow in soils polluted by the agents suggested at the end of investigation 1.

3. Pupils should obtain pictures of land showing various kinds of defacement and destruction of soil. Encourage personal photography, though pictures from magazines and newspapers can be used. A sanitary land fill, an open-pit mine, a rock quarry, and an automobile junk pile offer examples of land taken from production by pollution or waste disposal.

4. Each pupil should keep a record of the amount of solid waste produced by his family in one week. Calculate the total numbers of glass bottles, milk cartons, cardboard boxes, and so on, discarded by the families of the class during one week's time. Then compare the results with the estimated one ton of packages per family per year. Which of these waste products are made of materials that could be reused? Which waste products might be disposed of by other means than those used in your city?

5. Write to Public Affairs Department, Glass Container Manufacturers Institute, 330 Madison Avenue, New York, New York 10017, and ask how you can participate in a plan to salvage an estimated 11 billion bottles a year from the nation's litter. This project can lead to profits for a class project, as well as to reduction in refuse.

Sound Pollution

1. Identify all sounds heard during a period of twenty-four hours. Pupils should thus become more conscious of sounds and their sources. Construct an intensity scale on which students can classify sounds

from soft to extremely loud. Put these data in tabular form. What sounds seem more likely to be damaging to your ears?

2. Make a list of sounds that occur in your community. Classify them as "disturbing" or "undisturbing."

3. Describe ways in which some sounds might be muffled or reduced.

4. Investigate the differences between noise and "useful sounds." Prepare demonstrations of each. Have a musician show how music can be pleasing, whereas noise is disturbing.

5. Strike a tin can, metal tub, piece of pipe, or any other object that will reverberate, creating a loud noise in the classroom. How does this noise affect you?

6. Ask pupils to visit local businesses and industries that produce excessive noise in their operations. They should talk to owners or managers and find out whether or not steps are being taken to control noise.

7. Go into a room that does not have draperies, carpets, or acoustical ceiling—a room barren except for desks and chairs. Try making different kinds of noise, and observe how they reverberate. Try to make similar noises in a room with carpeting, draperies, and an acoustical ceiling, if possible. Do you notice any difference between the noises in these two rooms? Where does the noise go in a sound-insulated room? What might be done in public buildings and manufacturing plants to reduce noise levels?

TEACHING RESOURCES

U.S. Public Health Service Publication No. 1264 describes free films on air pollution that can be ordered from the U.S. Government Printing Office, Washington, D.C. 20402. The price is 15 cents. Sixteen 16-millimeter films and two 35-millimeter filmstrips are available.

Environmental Education. These 16-millimeter films are available from McGraw-Hill Films, 330 W. 42nd St., New York, New York 10036.

Air Pollution: Take a Deep Deadly Breath, 54 min, color.

The First Mile Up, 28 min, black and white.

The Silent Spring of Rachel Carson, 54 min, black and white.

Poisons, Pests, and People, on chemical insecticides and other means of controlling specific insects, 58 min, black and white.

The Problem with Water Is People, 30 min, color.

Water—Old Problems, New Approaches, 30 min, color.

The Dam Builders, 30 min, color.

Life Filmstrips' pollution series is available from Life Education Program, Box 834, Radio City Post Office, New York, New York 10019.
Part I: *The Great Lakes: History and Ecology*
Part II: *The Great Lakes: The Causes of Pollution*
Part III: *The Great Lakes: The Results of Pollution*

REFERENCES

Breysse, Peter A. "Sound Pollution—Another Urban Problem," *Science Teacher,* 37:29–34, April 1970.

Burns, William. *Noise and Man.* Philadelphia: Lippincott, 1969.

Carr, Donald E. *The Breath of Life.* New York: Norton, 1965.

Carson, Rachel. *Silent Spring.* Boston: Houghton Mifflin, 1962.

Carter, L. J. "Thermal Pollution: A Threat to Cayuga's Waters," *Science,* 163:517–518, February 7, 1969.

Clark, J. R. "Thermal Pollution and Aquatic Life," *Scientific American,* 220:18–27, March 1969.

Commoner, Barry. "Soil and Fresh Water: Damaged Global Fabric," *Environment,* 12:4–11, April 1970.

Edwards, Clive A. "Soil Pollutants and Soil Animals," *Scientific American,* 220:88–99, April 1969.

Epel, David & W. L. Lee, "Persistent Chemicals in the Marine Ecosystem," *American Biology Teacher,* 32:207–212, April 1970.

Graham, Frank, Jr. *Since Silent Spring.* Boston: Houghton Mifflin, 1970.

Kiesler, Hans. "Children Can Test for Water Pollution," *Instructor,* 78:93, May 1969.

Lindsay, Salby. "How Safe Is the Nation's Drinking Water?" *Saturday Review,* 53:54–55, May 2, 1970.

Lave, Lester B. & Eugene P. Seskin. "Air Pollution and Human Health," *Science,* 169:723–731, August 21, 1970.

McCullough, David G. "The Lonely War of a Good Angry Man," *American Heritage,* 21:97–113, December 1969.

McDermott, Walsh. "Air Pollution," *Scientific American,* 205:49–57, October 1961.

Merriman, Daniel. "The Calefaction of a River," *Scientific American,* 222:42–52, May 1970.

Nikolaieff, George A. *The Water Crisis.* New York: Wilson, 1967.

"Noise—Fourth Form of Pollution," *Environmental Science and Technology,* 4:720, September 1970.

Noise—Sound without Value. Committee on Environmental Quality of the Federal Council for Science and Technology. Washington, D.C.: Government Printing Office, 1968, p. 32.

"Our National Environmental Quotient," *National Wildlife,* 7:3–13, August–September 1969.

Renn, Charles E. *A Study of Water Quality*. Chestertown, Md.: Lamotte Chemical Products, 1968.

"Sources of Air Pollution and Their Control," *U.S. Public Health Service* Publication No. 1548. Washington, D.C.: Government Printing Office, 1968.

Taylor, Gordon Rattray. "The Threat to Life in the Sea," *Saturday Review,* 53:40–42, August 1, 1970.

chapter 6 / conservation of the environment

When European settlers first landed on the shores of America, their immediate and chief concern was survival in a hostile natural environment. Among an abundance of trees, it was necessary and even desirable to cut some down for shelter. Wild animals were usually plentiful and invaluable for their meat and fur. Any land that could be cleared was a gain in the struggle for survival. Spanish, English, and French alike showed little concern for their legacy to future generations. As a result of this understandable lack of vision, natural resources were squandered. Land was pillaged, wildlife was exterminated or endangered, and permanent damage was wreaked on many forms of plant life.

The Indians who had lived for centuries on the North American continent had disturbed the ecosystem little, maintaining balanced plant and animal communities. The deciduous forests of North America were a friendly part of the Indians' environment. They hunted deer, fowl, bear, squirrel, and rabbit; they ate wild berries, the roots of trees and plants, and nuts. But little that they did disturbed the balance of nature around them.

The white man's agriculture and industry, on the other hand, vastly upset the ecological balance. Cutting down trees, killing animals, destroying plants and depleting soil nutrients through cultivation seriously altered the balance that had existed for centuries.

Although man is the dominant species on earth, his reckless disregard for other animals and plants may threaten his own survival. No other species can consider or affect its own destiny; for the first time in history one species can knowingly make conscious decisions that can affect the numbers and variety of all other species.

A look at the food chain in a fresh-water ecosystem shows how higher animals derive their energy from animals and plants lower in the chain. All of the solar energy used by living organisms on the earth is converted through the process of photosynthesis into organic matter. Algae and green plants are the only organisms capable of doing this and are called producers. All organisms higher in the food chain are consumers and depend upon producers for their survival. Algae, as producers, feed small fish (primary consumers), which are in turn eaten by larger fish (secondary consumers). Large fish may be eaten by man. It is estimated that 10,000 kilograms of producers at the lowest level of this food chain are needed to produce 1 kilogram of weight on a man (Biological Sciences Curriculum Study, 1968).

Instilling appreciation of man's utter dependence upon the many animals and plants in his ecosystem should be a basic objective of elementary education. Development of conservation consciousness must be an integral part of the school curriculum. Teachers must exemplify in their own behavior a definite philosophy of and ethical regard for the environment. Conservation of both renewable and unrenewable resources is fundamental to man's continued survival on the spaceship called "earth."

Mineral resources, energy resources, soil nutrients, endangered animal species, wilderness areas, salt marshes, forest preserves, and outdoor recreation areas all involve aspects of conservation that must be analyzed.

SCIENTIFIC ATTITUDES

Despite all the information on pollution and conservation being published, children experience much uncertainty over what to believe. Conflicting arguments over the construction of a jetport in the Florida Everglades and its likely effects on the surrounding ecosystem, the consequences of building an oil pipeline across Alaska, and the effects of DDT on human health are examples in which reasoned judgment and emotional appeals compete. Emotionalism has won some important conservation battles, the consequence of which may be long-range harm to mankind. Amid all the charges and countercharges between conservationists and promoters of business interests children must have sound leadership if they are to reach reasonable decisions.

The development of scientific attitudes and sound reasoning remains a basic objective of elementary-school teaching. Consciousness of the environment does not permit protection of one resource at the expense of another that may contribute to human welfare. Children must learn to live and make decisions in a scientific way. Beside demonstrating curiosity and rationality the science student must be open-minded, willing to suspend judgment until enough available evidence has been carefully assessed. Intellectual honesty requires resistance to emotional expressions, especially when disguised as objectivity. Children should develop humility and respect for the natural world, as well as recognition of individual limitations and the limitations of the ecosystem.

A common classroom mistake is to spend a period investigating certain events and then drawing conclusions from the "experiment" conducted. A distinction should be made between a scientific experiment and the daily investigations that take place in an elementary-school classroom. An experiment is a long-range study of a specific problem, with controls on some variables. Before any valid conclusions can be reached, the experiment must be repeated several times without serious variation in results. In class children investigate phenomena and learn new insights. The processes of observing, communicating, and keeping records are important at this level. Only at higher levels of investigation should children be encouraged to make predictions and to draw inferences.

In order to demonstrate how public opinion can be influenced by individuals and organizations with particular interests or objectives, we shall examine the controversies over DDT, the Alaskan oil pipeline, and the Florida Everglades jetport. We do not intend to reach final conclusions or to pass judgment on what is right and wrong. Decision making must be based on sound scientific attitudes, and priorities according to human well-being must be established.

DDT: Friend or Foe?

Dichloro-diphenyl-trichloro-ethane (DDT) has been used to protect crops from disease-bearing insects and to control malaria-carrying mosquitoes and has thus contributed to the health and well-being of millions of people throughout the world in the past thirty years. Marcolino B. Candau, Director General of the World Health Organization, has reported that 3.5 million deaths from malaria were recorded annually in the early 1950s, whereas in 1966 there were fewer than one-third that many. In Ceylon the death rate of 20.1 per 1,000 was down to 9.1 per 1,000 in 1960, mainly because malaria had been nearly eradicated (Williams, 1969).

During the late 1960s, however, scientists and others concerned about the biological and ecological effects of DDT hammered away steadily at its continued use. After the pioneering work of Carson (1962) in indicting DDT as an enemy of nature, more and more evidence emerged to indicate that the continued use of this persistent pesticide is dangerous. Chlorinated hydrocarbons, of which DDT is one, remain essentially unchanged after their release into the environment, and they may thus have harmful effects thousands of miles away and years later. Evidence of concentrations of DDT (more than nineteen parts per million) in Coho salmon caught in Lake Michigan has led to prohibition of the sale of these fish for food.

The position of an animal in the food chain is one determinant of the DDT concentration in its body. The higher it is in the chain, the greater is the concentration. Plankton, one of the lowest forms of life in the ocean, absorb DDT. Krill, small shrimp-like creatures, eat the plankton. The concentration of DDT in penguins, which are higher on the food chain, is greater than is the concentration in krill.

Clear Lake, California, was sprayed with DDT for gnat control. Microscopic life there contained five parts per million of DDT. Fish feeding on these organisms had concentrations as high as 2,000 parts per million. Birds that fed on the fish died in great numbers, indicating that their DDT concentrations were much higher still (Keller, 1970).

Declining populations of hawks, eagles, and peregrine falcons—whose eggshells have become so thin that the eggs break before the birds can be hatched—have been attributed to increased concentrations of DDT and related insecticides in their bodies. Direct evidence of the ill effects upon man has not been reported, though we must remember that man stands at the top of the food chain. High concentrations of DDT in human milk have been reported.

In January 1971 the U.S. Court of Appeals in Washington ordered the Environmental Protection Agency to cancel all uses of DDT. Since that order was issued, the EPA has been conducting hearings on the use of DDT and has delayed ordering an immediate ban. It is believed that an abrupt suspension would force pesticide users to resort to other products that have not been fully evaluated and could be more dangerous than DDT.

The Alaskan Oil Pipeline

The discovery of vast deposits of oil at Prudhoe Bay on the North Slope of Alaska and subsequent plans to build a giant forty-eight-inch pipeline 800 miles south across the frozen tundra to the ice-free port of Valdez have aroused strong opposition among conservation groups, which claim that the pipeline should not be built until hazards to the environment have been carefully evaluated. This remote and virtually uninhabited land has become symbolic of a situation that is becoming more and more frequent. Can the insatiable appetite of an industrial economy be satisfied without destroying the few unspoiled wilderness areas left on earth? The North Slope sustains enormous herds of caribou, at least 440,000 or more. Their migrations are a dramatic part of the seasonal rhythm. Polar bears, timber wolves, wolverines, sheep, grizzly bears, and snowy owls also inhabit the region. The proposed pipeline would pump hot oil at a starting temperature of 160 degrees Fahrenheit, which would melt a ring of permafrost to a possible radius of twenty-five feet around the pipeline. Permafrost is the permanently frozen ground that lies a foot below the surface of the tundra, sometimes extending as deep as 1,300 feet; it keeps surface water from being absorbed into the subsoil. Melting this permanently frozen ground would result in a quagmire and possible soil erosion, with drastic effects on the ecosystem.

Even the strongest opponents recognize that these enormous quantities of oil will have to be extracted and transported to market; their opposition centers on potential damage to the physical environment and thus to regional wildlife from the specific *means* of extraction and transportation. A pipeline four feet in diameter built on stilts holding it two feet or more off the ground might block the migratory paths of caribou. A break in the line would release vast quantities of oil onto the landscape; one mile of the pipe would hold 500,000 gallons of oil.

Another issue is the potential effects of oil income on the Alaskan economy. Those who have subsisted on the resources of the land, often with little or no education for their children and limited medical and dental care, are potential recipients of tremendous financial benefits. The average resident of the North Slope has a fourth-grade education; one out of five Eskimos has never attended school. Tuberculosis rates are twenty times as high as those of the continental United States (Sullivan, 1970).

The Everglades Jetport

A prolonged and heated battle has been waged over the efforts of the City of Miami, Florida, to build a giant jetport on a thirty-nine-square-mile tract of Big Cypress Swamp just north of the Everglades. Conservationists, bent on preserving this natural wilderness area, have been pitted against promoters of the project, who envision the greatest jetport in the world, capable of handling international flights.

Although the issue has not yet been finally settled, on November 25, 1969, the Federal government forbade construction of the jetport. An arrangement was reached by which the training strip already built may be used by airline companies to train pilots until another location can be found. Then the land is to be ceded to the government and permitted to return to its natural state. President Richard M. Nixon has commented that this controversy has shown that the development of facilities like jetports "may have widespread environmental and social consequences that cannot wisely be left entirely to local initiative and local decision" (Bloomfield, 1970).

The Environmental Studies Board of the National Academy of Sciences had reported a study conducted in August 1969; it had noted that full-scale development of a jetport near the Everglades could have disastrous consequences unless industrial and residential development were kept to a minimum and adequate water-resources management were practiced (Mueller, 1969). This group had specified that a natural water-conservation area is absolutely essential to the future life of Everglades National Park and also to population development along the coastal areas of southwest Florida.

The Everglades National Park is basically a vast, shallow, slow-moving river through which fresh water moves seventy miles south and southwest from the region of Lake Okeechobee to the northern boundary of the park. Construction of the proposed jetport would release around 5.5 million gallons of sewage and industrial waste a day. The teeming subtropical plant and animal life in the park and north of it make the Everglades a biological laboratory, a spectacular display of wading birds, alligators, and fish. Eight species of birds, including the roseate spoonbill, the egret, the wood stork, and the ibis, nest in the park. If the water supply to the Everglades were severely reduced or contaminated, it would be fatal to wildlife.

All current issues related to the environment are incorporated in the struggle to preserve the primitive condition of the Everglades while permitting the scientific and technological advances that man has traditionally considered progress. The challenge to all citizens when a natural ecosystem is threatened and nature is being abused is to find ways to work together, to compromise selfish interests, and to weigh the benefits and the risks involved in proposed change. In many matters affecting the ecological balance man is going to have to change his life style, accepting some sacrifices for long-range benefits to future generations.

CONSERVATION PAST AND PRESENT

History

Serious concern about management of land, water, and forestry resources in the United States has only appeared recently in our nation's history. Among those who have been prominently associated with development of national conservation policy are Theodore Roosevelt, Gifford Pinchot, John Muir, John Wesley Powell, and Franklin Delano Roosevelt. Theodore Roosevelt focused national attention on conservation during his two terms of office, 1900–1908. He attempted to create a national conservation policy, with the assistance of one of the few trained foresters in the United States, Gifford Pinchot, whom Roosevelt had appointed to organize the U.S. Forest Service. It was Pinchot who first applied the term "conservation" to this effort, in 1907, in connection with forestry-management practices; it was derived from the "conservancies," or government forests, in India (Zurhorst, 1970).

An eminent explorer, geologist, and conservationist was John Wesley Powell. His most spectacular accomplishment was an expedition down the Colorado River, which covered more than 900 miles in nearly three months. This epic journey made him a national hero, but it was his continuing work in the arid lands of the United States that led to passage of laws defining rights to water, grazing, and exploitation of the public domain. Powell was instrumental in founding the U.S. Geological Survey, which mapped and surveyed the vast western regions of the country. Especially he should be remembered for his efforts to influence Federal policies on the public domain.

Long before the word "ecology" became part of the common language of naturalists, John Muir had noted that, when one "layer" of nature is disturbed in a given area, effects are transmitted to other "areas," often with far-reaching consequences. From 1869 to 1914 he tramped every trail in the Sierra Mountains, from south to north, studying geology, mapping streams, and listing flowers. His thoughtful observations, original mind, and clear writing were all pressed into service to save fine bits of America's scenic heritage. The Sierra Club, which Muir helped to found in 1892, still perpetuates his interest in exploration, enjoyment, and protection of national scenic resources.

Concern about national conservation policies seems then to have been sidetracked by other national problems until the early 1930s. Then damaging floods on major rivers, the spreading blight of rural poverty, and the vast devastation of the Dust Bowl in the Great Plains demanded drastic new approaches to conservation. When, under the administration of Franklin Roosevelt beginning in 1933, a second wave of enthusiasm for conservation swelled, it generated lively congressional support. The Civilian Conservation Corps (C.C.C.) and the Tennessee Valley Authority (T.V.A.) were established; both were designed to improve the social and economic circumstances of many people during the Depression years. The C.C.C. provided work for unemployed men planting trees, building small dams, and taking other measures to arrest soil erosion.

The Soil Conservation Service, another landmark in the national conservation movement, was created in 1935. During the second Roosevelt era the cause of conservation thus became a national one; the wise use of land and its products was to benefit all citizens of the United States.

In the 1960s interest in conservation and other aspects of the environment revived once again. A look at some leading conservation organizations impresses us with the magnitude of recent interest in this field.

Conservation Organizations

Many powerful and effective organizations are interested in the environment, conservation, population, and specific aspects of environmental problems. Organizations like the Sierra Club, the National Audubon Society, and the National Wildlife Federation have in recent years gained national and international recognition for their relentless stands on many environmental questions. The Sierra Club has been involved in battles to protect natural resources in many parts of the country in recent years. Thirty chapters are now affiliated with the national organization from coast to coast.

The National Wildlife Federation, with a membership of more than 400,000, is the largest of these organizations. Its publications, *National Wildlife* and *Ranger Rick* (for children) are useful for school and home.

Concern about egrets that were being hunted for their plumage in the Florida Everglades in 1905 led to foundation of the National Audubon Society, which is now active in many other aspects of environmental protection. *Audubon* and *Audubon Nature Bulletins* (for teachers and youth leaders) are excellent for school use. This society also supports Audubon Wildlife Films, Audubon Camps, and Audubon Centers, to which children and their teachers come for personal contact with nature.

These organizations are only 3 of more than 250 listed in *Conservation Directory*, also published by the National Wildlife Federation. There are also many state and local groups with similar purposes. A more complete list of environmental organizations that may be of value to teachers is provided in Appendix A.

Some significant accomplishments have been won by the environmental organizations in recent years. The Environmental Defense Fund, a scientific organization established in 1967 and dedicated to use of the courts for environmental protection, has been instrumental in initiating suits and petitions against users of "hard" pesticides. The Audubon Society and the Sierra Club have sued to delay construction of the Everglades jetport and to protect the barge canal across Florida. Recent defeat in Congress of continued funding for the supersonic transport (SST) was the direct fruit of efforts by about thirty organizations that formed the Coalition Against the SST. The fight against continued use of DDT and other persistent pesticides has been pursued by many environmental organizations, and it led to a ban on almost all further use of DDT after January 1971.

Federal Agencies

The National Environmental Policy Act was passed on January 1, 1970; it spelled out national policy on the environment and created the Council on Environmental Quality in the executive branch of the Federal government. Federal agencies are now required to make detailed reports on any of their activities that significantly affect the quality of the human environment. The council has authority to oversee, as well as to develop new policies for, protection of the environment.

Creation of the Environmental Protection Agency in December 1970 was one of the first major accomplishments of the Council on Environmental Quality. The E.P.A. combines programs formerly spread among many Federal agencies:

1. The Federal Water Quality Administration.
2. The National Air Pollution Control Administration.
3. Pesticide-research authority from the Department of the Interior.
4. Pesticide-research and standard-setting programs of the Food and Drug Administration.
5. General ecological-research authority from the Council on Environmental Quality.
6. The environmental radiation-standards program of the Atomic Energy Commission.
7. The pesticides-registration program of the Agricultural Research Service.

Many agencies in the nine departments of the executive branch, as well as several independent government agencies, are nevertheless involved in administration and study of environmental programs. Certainly the creation of the Environmental Protection Agency will eventually help to consolidate many of these efforts also. The President's environmental program for 1971 included proposals for legislation to deal with sulfur-oxide emissions, a tax on lead in gasoline, waste-treatment facilities, water-quality standards and enforcement, pesticides, recycling wastes, toxic substances, ocean dumping, noise, national land-use policy, siting of power plants, and protection of mining lands. These environmental problems are some of those identified by the Council on Environmental Quality as requiring congressional action. By far the most significant recent legislation has been the enactment of the Clean Air Act of 1970; it requires that emissions of hydrocarbons, carbon monoxide, and nitrogen oxide from 1975 model cars be reduced to 90 percent below those permitted from 1970 models.

CRITICAL AREAS

Endangered Species

The whooping crane stood on the brink of complete extinction only a few years ago, but careful planning and stringent protection of its habitat have slowly increased its numbers once again. During the first century after the discovery of this continent cranes were evidently fairly numerous along the Atlantic coast from Florida to New England. The whooping crane stands about five feet tall when stretched to its full height and is conspicuous by its white color. It occupied only the open lands and was soon driven out when settlement began. Today at the Patuxent Wildlife Research Station near Laurel, Maryland, twenty-one whooping cranes are being reared in captivity. The remaining, wild members of the species winter along the Texas Gulf Coast and migrate to Canada for their breeding season during the summer. Last winter fifty-six birds were counted at the wintering grounds at the Arkansas Wildlife Refuge (Phillips, 1970). The story of how biologists and naturalists have rescued this rare and beautiful bird from extinction is a moving example of how man can protect his friends, the flora and fauna, when he is aroused to the danger.

The American bald eagle, peregrine falcon, brown pelican, sea otter, black-footed ferret, alligator, California condor, blue whale, and ivory-billed woodpecker are other species that are now rare or in danger of extinction. The ivory-billed woodpecker is perhaps already extinct. Altogether thirty-two mammals, sixty birds, twelve reptiles and amphibians, and thirty-eight fish species are listed as "rare and endangered" in "Rare and Endangered Fish and Wildlife of the United States," prepared by the U.S. Bureau of Sport Fisheries and Wildlife (1968). Many other species whose statuses are indeterminate or peripheral are also included in this publication. An endangered species is defined as "one whose prospects for survival and reproduction are in immediate jeopardy" ("Rare and Endangered Fish and Wildlife of the United States," 1968, ii).

The skins and furs of many wild animals from both the United States and foreign countries are used to make coats, shoes, and handbags. New York state has banned the sale of all alligator and crocodile products, as well as products made from leopards, tigers, cheetahs, vicuñas, red wolves, polar bears, and mountain lions. California has recently enacted a similar law that omits the mountain lion, though it does include the sea otter.

Why should such great efforts be expended to preserve animals like the Texas kangaroo rat, the Hawaiian crow, and the dusky-seaside sparrow? These and many other endangered fauna are unknown to most people in the world, but their protection is essential to the welfare of our society. Extinct animals, like lost time, can never be recovered. The value of an individual species may not be known, but this very fact is an important reason for trying to keep it alive. Alteration of the ecosystem in which a species lives is the principal cause of extinction. Loss of one or more species might equally disrupt an ecosystem. Man's survival on this planet depends upon the ecological balance of the universal ecosystem. Just as he has contributed to extinction of animals that were once part of our ecosystem—the plains wolf, the passenger pigeon, the heath hen, and the dodo bird—so he must now work to preserve the remaining species. Otherwise he himself may become an endangered species.

Estuaries and Tidal Marshes

Around the coastline of the United States, from Maine to the Texas Gulf and from Washington State to southern California are the bays, inlets, river mouths, lagoons, and tidal marshes that constitute the "interface" between land drainage and the oceans. Each estuary is a unique ecosystem, with its own inhabitants and pollution problem (Cronin, 1970). Through evolutionary selection and adaptation certain species have successfully acclimated themselves to habitation of particular estuaries.

Estuaries are the places where fresh water comes in contact with salt water, which creates variations in salinity, temperature fluctuations, high turbidity, and other environmental stresses. Tidal marshes are areas of boggy, peat-like ground built up around the borders of estuaries over periods of years. They are periodically inundated by ocean or bay tides. Grasses, ranging from short cord and eel grasses to tall, reedy cattails and foxtails, grow in these salt marshes. Abundant salt hay was once gathered by early settlers for livestock feed. Most commercially important fish and shellfish depend upon these marshes at some stage in their life histories. Blue crabs, shrimp, and oysters use the marshes as nurseries; young shrimp spend three months there before leaving for the open sea.

Mammals and other land animals also live there and feed on the plants and animals found there. Muskrats, otters, raccoons, foxes, mink, rabbits, and weasels all thrive in salt marshes. Ducks, geese, and coots feed on waterbugs, beetles, dragonflies, and damselflies. Salamanders and crayfish burrow in the silt and mud.

The human use of estuaries—filling in salt marshes for land development, diverting water from major river systems to supply urban areas, dumping pollutants into bays and rivers, and mining bays—threatens their survival and the survival of life in them. In San Francisco Bay 300 square miles of the original 700 square miles have been filled to provide land for industry, commerce, and homes (Marx, 1970). The disruption of estuaries that prevents even one species from continuing there may completely alter a food chain leading up to man's vital source of seafood. Grass stalks wither and die in a salt marsh each winter, contributing nutrients to the water as they decompose and decay. Microscopic animals feed on these nutrients and are eaten in turn by oysters, shrimp, clams, and scallops. Some of these animals are consumed by crabs, larger fish, waterfowl, and water mammals. Man eats many of these larger two groups of animals.

Management of coastal zones is required. Development of marshes and estuaries has been largely controlled by private enterprise, for public needs have remained undefined, and national and state policies have been nonexistent. Policies must be developed in the public interest, to protect areas like Bald Head Island, North Carolina; Hilton Head Island, South Carolina; Biscayne Bay, Florida; and many others. It is estimated that between 800 and 900 estuaries exist along our coastline, all of them in danger of abuse and destruction unless ample measures are taken to ensure their continuation undisturbed. Understanding the importance of preserving these focal points while recognizing that man's aspirations must also be fulfilled can lead to satisfactory compromises.

Energy Resources

In the United States the insatiable appetite for energy to run factories, commercial establishments, transportation systems, and personal appliances has resulted in an energy-consumption growth rate of 5 percent a year since 1965. The enormous demands for energy in all forms has resulted in two problems of increasing magnitude. First, the supply of energy available, whether it be from coal, oil, natural gas, or uranium, is finite and will eventually be exhausted unless conservation is practiced. Second, the increased consumption of fossil fuels, primarily to produce electric energy, has resulted in dumping of wastes to the point at which the environment is being seriously taxed to absorb all of them. These two problems can both be said to be approaching crisis level.

When we examine the problem of energy supply and demand we find a short-term crisis, in that power companies are not able to supply energy as rapidly as the growing population is demanding it. In 1970 electricity requirements to operate air conditioners, washing machines, dishwashers, toothbrushes, escalators, television sets, and endless other common appliances in this affluent society approached 8,000 kilowatt-hours per person annually. Electric-power production is now doubling every ten years.

One reason for this crisis has been delays in construction of planned electrical generating plants because of opposition from environmental groups, which have demanded that companies produce "cleaner" smoke, keep down thermal pollution of water supplies, and show regard for the aesthetic aspects of the environment. Many cities, including New York City, have recently ruled that no coal containing more than 1 percent sulfur can be burned. As more than 50 percent of the fuel for electric-power plants is coal typically containing 2–3 percent sulfur, the use of coal has been curtailed.

One example of the delays that have been caused is provided by the Consolidated Edison Company's effort to construct a hydroelectric plant on Storm King Mountain to supply electric energy to the New York City area. The plant was first proposed in 1963 as a gigantic facility that would draw 18,000 cubic feet of water per second from the Hudson River near Cornwall, fifty miles north of New York City. Conservationists were concerned about effects on more than fifty species of marine and freshwater fish that inhabit the Hudson. Many of these species spawn in the river, which is classed as an estuary from its mouth up to the Troy dam, 150 miles north. After long litigation the Storm King Mountain plant has not yet been built, and the present tight power situation in New York City and the surrounding area is attributed by some people to this lengthy delay.

The switch from coal has necessitated greater use of fuel oil or natural gas, neither of which is abundantly available in the United States. Fuel oil is obtained from Venezuela, Libya, and the Arabian oil fields, but political unrest has limited imports from these sources. Natural gas is just not obtainable in large quantities.

Nuclear-powered generating plants are a possible long-range solution to the nation's energy needs. Nuclear reactors are most seriously criticized because of their thermal pollution of water and possible radiation pollution. In the early 1960s nuclear energy was looked on as holding a great deal of promise for generating electric power, but construction of plants has not been nearly as rapid as had been expected, because of environmental concerns and production problems. When we consider the risks to the public from nuclear-powered plants, we should compare them with present hazards from fossil-fuel power plants that would be eliminated.

Underground steam as a source of energy has recently been the subject of intensive investigation by a group of scientists at the Riverside campus of the University of California. Robert Rex, director of the Institute of Geophysics and Planetary Physics there, is one of the leaders of an effort to revolutionize the economy of the American Southwest through the use of geothermal steam (Lear, 1970). A vast underground sponge of porous rock saturated with brine is heated to boiling temperatures by conduction from the solid rock below it. Under that solid rock lies congealing magma, pushed up from the earth's interior by an overturning of the floor of the Pacific Ocean. This overturning occurs on all the ocean floors. On the bottom of the Pacific Ocean is a domed blister that has pushed its way under the North American continent. The pressure of this dome has been slowly tearing away the segment of the continent lying west of the San Andreas fault, and heat produced escapes through hot springs all over the American West. The government of Mexico has begun installing specially designed turbines that will convert underground steam into electric power by the summer of 1972.

Geothermal power might be a solution to some of the difficulties that electric-power companies have experienced, including that of sulfur oxides emitted from oil- or coal-burning furnaces. It can be harnessed more cheaply and does not have the damaging effects on the environment that fossil-fuel or nuclear electrical generators produce. Areas in which there are known thermal springs exist all through California, Washington, Oregon, Idaho, Montana, Wyoming, Utah, Colorado, New Mexico, Arizona, and Nevada, as well as in Mexico. Geysers like Old Faithful at Yellowstone National Park are points of extreme geothermal activity.

Geothermal steam has been used to heat homes in Iceland since 1925; New Zealand has made extensive use of such steam to produce electrical energy. Some instances in which it has been used in the United States include heating of houses in Boise, Idaho, by steam that has been issuing from the earth since 1890. The Geysers, a geothermal steam field ninety miles north of San Francisco, has a series of "fumaroles" from which steam pours; it is used to generate electricity.

Concerned environmentalists must seek solutions to the conflict between the overwhelming forces of demand for energy and attempts to control production of energy because it damages the environment. One thing is certain: We must learn to live with constantly increasing energy consumption. Whether or not we can adjust our means of production to protect the environment will determine our ability to survive over the long term.

The Committee for Environmental Information, a St. Louis corporation, has suggested several ecological measures to reduce consumption of electric energy. Recycling waste paper would curtail heavy demands for electricity in paper production. Automobiles that could be easily and economically reclaimed would reduce energy requirements for producing steel and at the same time would solve the problem of junked cars. To make a ton of steel plate or wire from ore requires energy equivalent to 2,700 kilowatt-hours, whereas reclaimed steel from an electric furnace requires only 700 kilowatt-hours a ton. Aluminum factories use a great deal of electrical energy, as do factories making nitrogen fertilizers. Our living style must be adjusted to reduce consumption of these items ("The Space Available," 1970).

Individual decisions have a direct impact on conservation of energy: They should be based on common-sense judgments of sound practices in everyday living. Turning off lights; walking short distances instead of driving a car; learning to ride the bus instead of driving a car; being less wasteful of water; reusing paper bags for trash, rather than buying plastic containers; using worn-out clothes for dust cloths instead of buying paper dust cloths; and buying returnable bottles are some personal habits that should be adopted. Not only are they good for the environment, they also contribute to good health and the family budget.

In the grocery store convenience packaging has done much to make life easier for the housewife, but it has also contributed mightily to pollution and energy consumption. It is difficult to purchase an item today that is not packaged, though a consumer can seek out returnable packages. He can also inform himself about which materials are biodegradable and which are not. Plastics, which are being increasingly used in containers and packages, pose a serious threat because they are nonbiodegradable and tend to melt rather than to burn when incinerated. Polyvinyl-chloride plastic (P.V.C.) produces hydrochloric acid when burned. P.V.C. materials include most hard plastic containers, like milk cartons, *Clorox* bottles, and so on. Most plastic bags are polyethylene. The consumer has to be well informed and wise in order to recognize the personal benefits and to protect the environment.

Wilderness Areas

A national wilderness-preservation system was established in 1964 with the passage of the Wilderness Bill, which provides statutory protection for qualified lands in national forests, national parks and monuments, national wildlife refuges, and game range lands. The last two units added to the system—the Ventana Wilderness, in Los Padres National Forest south of Carmel, California, and the 63,500-acre Desolation Wilderness in the Sierra Nevada Mountains of California—bring the total to sixty-one units in the wilderness system. All the present wilderness areas are in western states, except for the Great Gulf Wilderness Area in New Hampshire, Linville Gorge and Shining Rock in North Carolina, and Boundary Waters Canoe Area in Minnesota.

According to the act, "A wilderness, in contrast to those areas where man and his own works dominate the landscape, is hereby recognized as an area where the earth and its community of life are untrammeled by man, and where man is a visitor who does not remain." Each wilderness area contains at least 5,000 acres of land unimpaired by permanent roads or other works of man.

One purpose of preserving wilderness areas is to set aside lands that man can visit without disturbing them. Gilligan (1963) has listed characteristics of wilderness areas:

1. Primary watershed protection.
2. Scientific research potential.
3. Essential habitats for many species of scarce plants and animals.
4. Pure air and water.
5. Reserves of important historical and cultural significance.
6. Sources of enjoyment and symbolic meaning to millions of human beings.

7. Relatively unmodified natural landscape offering spaciousness, beauty, and variety: key features of contrast with developed land areas.
8. Opportunity for recreation and outdoor activities: nature study, hiking, climbing, skiing, boating, camping, hunting, and fishing.
9. Opportunities for isolation, challenge, and refinement of sensory impressions.

Just as we must preserve wildlife for which there is no apparent use now, so we must maintain wilderness areas that have no direct material utility to man in the immediate present.

PROJECTS

Study of a Biotic Community

For fourth, fifth, and sixth grade children, a very satisfactory project involving the many facets of a biological community can be developed. Children can learn the basic scientific processes of observing, communicating, record keeping, organizing data, using numbers, hypothesizing, generalizing, and so on. While learning these processes they can also develop through actual experience understanding of communities, food chains and webs, interrelations, dependence, the balance of nature, succession in a community, adaptation, and other ecological concepts. They can begin to understand relations among species, the relative "importance" of various species, and the structure of the community.

As different schools have different kinds of communities available for study, the teacher and the class should work out procedures most convenient for their own. The main objective is to observe the organisms that live in an active natural community. There are five steps to be followed. First, a study site should be selected. Second, it should be decided what kind of data to collect. Third, the particular area to be studied should be measured; it can be ten square meters of forest or one square meter of a cultivated field. Fourth, the data should be collected, and a form for accurate recording should be selected. This step offers a good opportunity to introduce the construction and use of graphs. Finally, the data should be analyzed in school, where secondary source materials and time are available.

Some problems for investigation include

1. What kind of community is available for study: a forest, a natural prairie, a cultivated area, a lawn with planted trees and shrubs, a body of water?

2. Would a vacant lot covered with weeds, brush, and debris be a biotic community worth studying?

3. What kinds of data will be collected? Will one community be compared with another, or will data be collected from only one community?

4. What procedures are to be used in identifying organisms? Elementary-school children should not necessarily have to learn family and species names, but they should learn general group names.

5. Will the study involve quantitative information—how many, how long, what weight, and so on? How will measurements be made? (Teachers should practice using metric measurements, so that children can learn to work with centimeters, meters, liters, milliliters, and so on, instead of inches, feet, quarts, pints, and the like.)

6. What is a plant or animal's niche or place and function in the community? Is it a producer like plants that convert solar energy into chemical energy? Is it a primary consumer like insects, rodents, some birds, rabbits, and deer? Is it a secondary consumer like lizards, snakes, frogs, and toads? Is it a tertiary consumer like foxes, hawks, and hyenas? Is it a scavenger or saprovore like termites, earthworms, maggots, buzzards, and vultures? Is it a decomposer like bacteria, yeasts, and molds?

7. Can a food chain or food web of the species in the community be described?

8. Can the "job" of each species in the community be identified?

9. Students should list possible changes that might occur if certain species were removed from the community.

10. What effects could air pollution, water pollution, and soil pollution have on species in this community? Students should list species that are harmed by particular types of pollution that occur in this community.

Developing a Site for Conservation and Outdoor Education

A school's long-range planning program should include development of a laboratory for outdoor education. Many inner-city and other urban schools are built on limited land areas, which necessitate even more careful planning of school property and incorporation of as many types of environments as possible. At an existing school adaptation of the grounds to include environmental-education sites must be considered; at a new school such sites should be planned from the beginning.

Some types of environments that may be controlled by the schools are

1. *Bare lands*. Paved areas, an eroding bank, or a field corner.
2. *Borders*.
3. *Courtyards*. With trees, shrubs, and grass.
4. *Elevations*. Slopes or hilltops.
5. *Forb lands*. Areas of herbaceous plants, either annual or perennial, other than grasses.
6. *Grasslands*. Lawns and turf for playing fields.
7. *Rough grass areas*.
8. *Odd areas and corners*.
9. *Shrubbery areas*. Building foundations, corners, facings, hedges and screens, special plantings, and brush lands.
10. *Wooded areas*. With shade trees, plantations, native woods.
11. *Water*. Lakes, ponds, puddles, streams.
12. *Wetlands*. Marshes, shrub swamps, swamps, and bogs. ("School Site Development for Conservation and Outdoor Education," 1969)

Every school system, whether just started or already established, should ask the advice of biologists, soil conservationists, naturalists, and landscape artists, as well as of its own teachers, administrators, and staff. Planning an outdoor laboratory requires imagination and a lot of work, but it can be most rewarding. One suburban school has fenced in an area between two wings of the building. A small spring originates in this area, which made it possible to develop a shrub swamp in one section, forb land in another section, and brush land in a third section of this small space. Possibilities for investigations in this outdoor laboratory are virtually unlimited.

An Investigation of Heat-Energy Transfer

How does insulating a house affect the amount of energy required to heat it in the winter and cool it in the summer?

The teacher can improvise two calorimeters, one well insulated and one uninsulated. The latter can be a pint jar with a thermometer mounted so that it measures the temperature in the center of the jar's contents. The former can be made from a styrofoam cup, with another cup inverted over it to hold the heat in. Equal quantities (100 cubic centimeters or more) of hot water should be put in each calorimeter. The thermometers should then be placed with their bulbs in the center of the water and not touching the sides or bottoms of the containers. Students should then take temperature readings at regular time intervals as the water cools. After about thirty minutes enough data should have been collected to permit preparation of a graph of the temperature readings.

This project involves observation, data collection, planning, hypothesizing, communicating, preparing graphs, using numbers, and inferring. Efforts might be made to examine heat loss through various types of insulating materials. Another approach involves using ice water in the calorimeters to see whether or not heat flow into the containers is affected by insulating materials in the same manner as is heat flow out of the containers. Pupils may also devise their own investigations of heat flow. They should be encouraged to learn how to define a problem and to organize an investigation of that problem.

This and similar projects should promote recognition that heat energy flows naturally from a warmer to a colder region (Second Law of Thermodynamics). They can be used also to develop understanding of the law of conservation of energy. Although energy may take different forms, the sum total of the energy in the universe is constant. Questions about matter-energy relations in nuclear reactions arise. If we remember that matter is a store of chemical energy, we can better understand the concept of conservation of energy.

Personal Involvement

Part of developing environmental awareness is development of new attitudes toward life and the bounties of nature. Children and adults are more likely to change their attitudes if they are personally involved in the decision-making process. Activities that should become part of daily activities at school include keeping lists of personal resolves for contribution to reducing pollution and furthering conservation. The following list can be used, added to, changed, and constantly updated:

1. Drive your car as little as possible. Try walking or cycling. Form car pools, or ride the bus or train.
2. Use less electricity. Consider disposing of luxury electrical gadgets like electric knives, toothbrushes, can openers, and self-cleaning ovens.
3. Practice turning off lights when they are not needed. Try smaller-watt bulbs in overhead light fixtures, but do not sacrifice eyesight to save electricity in reading lamps!
4. Keep the home heating system operating efficiently. Operate the thermostat at a slightly lower temperature while keeping the humidity at a comfortable level. It is generally agreed that 40–50 percent relative humidity with a temperature of 68–70 degrees Fahrenheit is optimal.

5. Conserve water. Put a brick or two in the tank of the toilet to reduce the amount of water used with each flushing. Become more conscious of the water that you use for washing and bathing. A tub bath generally requires more water than does a shower.

6. Consume less. Begin by reducing your personal overconsumption. Food, clothing, and luxury conveniences can all be saved.

7. Look for products that are not "convenience" packaged. Prepared foods and other packaged products cost more, and the packages must be disposed of.

8. Reduce the quantity of paper products—napkins, towels, cups, disposable plates, spoons, and so on—that you use.

9. Avoid using colored paper products, for the dyes increase the contamination of water.

10. Launder with washing soda and detergents that have few or no phosphates (see Appendix B).

11. Keep a compost heap of grass, leaves, garden clippings, and biodegradable garbage in your yard. Use this compost as a substitute for chemical fertilizers.

12. Use as little tinfoil, aluminum foil, and plastic as possible. They are not biodegradable.

13. Consider which of the bottled and packaged materials that you use can be recycled. Insist on returnable bottles, and reuse boxes and bags.

14. Do not use DDT or other persistent pesticides: aldrin, chlordane, dieldrin, endrin, heptachlor, lindane, benzene hexachloride, toxaphene, isodrin, and dilan. Find out which insects serve as natural pest controls; some of them are ladybugs, praying mantises, aphis lions, dragonflies, and ground beetles. Certain herbs and plants are also natural enemies of plant pests.

15. If you do not smoke, do not start. If you do, stop. Remember that the U.S. Surgeon General has announced that cigarette smoking endangers health.

16. Resolve to limit your future family size to two children.

17. Plant a tree. Encourage the growth of plants instead of more paving or concrete-walled areas.

18. Promote parks in your community.

19. Accept greater personal responsibility. Set an example. Demand action.

20. Deposit all litter in appropriate containers. Pick up litter. Let others see you picking it up; it is "catching."

21. Try to discourage such wasteful, unplanned use of land as spot

zoning, leapfrogging suburban development, urban sprawl, and destruction of aesthetic areas.

22. Strive to improve your understanding of environmental problems and issues, and help to inform others.

23. Start a vegetable garden. The produce can reduce your family's food budget, beside helping to develop the soil and its organisms.

24. Consider carefully buying any garments made from the furs or skins of animals. Do not buy anything made from endangered wild animals. Use furs of those animals that are raised commercially: minks, chinchillas, and rabbits. Or wear synthetic furs.

25. Separate your garbage into biodegradables, which can be used as fertilizer in your garden; paper products, which can be recycled; aluminum products, which can also be recycled; and the rest, which should go into sanitary land fill or other garbage disposal.

Involving and Influencing Other People

Writing, telephoning, and talking to various civic and business leaders provide opportunities to develop understanding of democratic processes, as well as language skills. Here are some suggestions:

1. Write to local businesses whose manufacturing or commercial processes contribute pollutants to air, water, or land. Ask for explanations of what the company is doing to curtail their pollution.

2. Find out about the sewage-treatment facilities in your community and how they are being adjusted to accommodate increased effluence.

3. Write to the city sanitation department for explanations of how solid wastes are disposed of and whether or not efforts are being made to reclaim land used for sanitary land fill.

4. Ask local officials about converting internal-combustion engines used by the city to fuels like natural gas that contribute less pollution.

5. Write to the U.S. Forestry Service for information about scientific forest management to minimize waste and to conserve soil and forest resources.

6. Write or call the local office of the U.S. Soil Conservation Service for information on protection of land from erosion and feeding of wildlife. Letting grass and grain go to seed along

ploughed terraces, highway right-of-ways, and fence rows provides feed for birds.

7. Inform the local newspaper of what your class is doing about pollution; inquire about other conservation efforts.

8. Write or call the electric-power company for information about how your electricity is generated. Electric-power plants are heavy polluters.

9. Write to your state representatives and senators for their views on environmental issues that affect your community.

10. Make contact with local conservation organizations, which need your support and are willing to assist schools in environmental causes.

11. Start a recycling program in your community. Write to the Glass Container Manufacturers Institute, 330 Madison Avenue, New York, New York 10017, to find out about their glass-reclamation program.

12. Collect magazines, newspapers, and other paper products. Take them to a waste-paper collection center.

13. Save all aluminum cans and packaging for recycling. If you do not know of an aluminum-reclamation center in your area write to Reynolds Aluminum Company, P.O. Box 2346LI, Richmond, Virginia 23218; or to Kaiser Aluminum and Chemical Corporation, 300 Lakeside Drive, Oakland, California 94604. (Aluminum cans have no side and bottom seams.)

14. Insist that antipollution laws be enforced.

15. Recognize companies that are working to solve recycling and other environmental problems. For example, the Coca-Cola Company has helped to set up in the New York, New Jersey, and Connecticut areas seventeen collection centers where glass and aluminum containers can be returned for cash. The Reynolds Aluminum Company initiated a reclamation program in the Los Angeles area that has now spread to other sections of the country.

REFERENCES

Abelson, Philip H. "Scarcity of Energy," *Science*, 169:1297, September 25, 1970.

Biological Sciences Curriculum Study. *Biological Science: An Inquiry into Life*, 2nd ed. New York: Harcourt, 1968.

Bloomfield, Howard. "The Everglades—Pregnant with Risk," *American Forests*, 76:24–27, May 1970.

Boffey, Philip M. "Energy Crises: Environmental Issue Exacerbates Power Supply Problem," *Science*, 168:1554–1559, June 26, 1970.

Brennan, Matthew J. (ed.). *People and Their Environment: Teachers' Curriculum Guides to Conservation Education.* 8 vols. Chicago: Ferguson, 1969.

Brooks, Paul. "Superjetport or Everglades Park?" *Audubon*, 71:4–11, July 1969.

Cailliet, Greg, Paulette Setzer & Milton Love. *Everyman's Guide to Ecological Living.* New York: Macmillan, 1971.

Carson, Rachel. *Silent Spring.* Boston: Houghton Mifflin, 1962.

Carter, Luther J. "North Slope: Oil Rush," *Science*, 166:85–92, October 3, 1969.

"Conservation for Sixth Graders," *American Forests*, 74:27–29, April 1968.

"Conservationists: Who Conserves What," *Changing Times*, 23:24–27, August 1969.

Cronin, L. Eugene. "The Test of the Estuaries," *Bioscience*, 20:3959, April 1970.

Dasmann, Raymond. *Environmental Conservation.* New York: Wiley, 1967.

Dorst, Jean. *Before Nature Dies.* Boston: Houghton Mifflin, 1960.

Ehrenfeld, David W. *Biological Conservation.* New York: Holt, 1970.

George, Jean. "From the Brink of Extinction," *National Wildlife*, 7:20–23, April 1969.

Gilligan, James R. "The Wilderness Resources," *Tomorrow's Wilderness,* François Leydet (ed.). San Francisco: Sierra Club, 1963.

"The Great Phosphorus Controversy," *Environmental Science and Technology,* 4:725–726, September 1970.

Gross, Edward. "Getting Set for a Black Gold Rush," *Science News*, 97:177–179, February 14, 1970.

Haney, Richard D. "The Development of Scientific Attitudes," in Edward Victor and Marjorie Lerner (eds.), *Readings in Science Education for the Elementary School.* New York: Macmillan, 1967, pp. 69–75.

Harrison, George H. "Yes, We Are Teaching Johnny Conservation," *National Wildlife*, 8:42–47, April 1970.

Jensen, Albert C. "Fish and Power Plants," *Conservationist*, 24:2–5, December 1969.

Keller, Eugenia. "The DDT Story," *Chemistry*, 43:8–12, February 1970.

LaBastille, Anne. "Conservation Careers for Women," *Conservationist*, 24:31–32, June–July 1970.

Laycock, George. "Kiss the North Slope Goodbye," *Audubon*, 72:68–74, September 1970.

Laycock, George. "Whittling Alaska Down to Size," *Audubon*, 71:77–78, May 1969.

Lear, John. "Clean Power from Inside the Earth," *Saturday Review*, 53:53–61, December 5, 1970.

Linton, Ron M. *Terracide—America's Destruction of Her Living Environment.* Boston: Little, Brown, 1970.

Marx, Wesley. "How To Rescue a Bay in Distress," *Oceans*, 3:34–41, September–October 1970.

Matthews, William H., III. "America's Open-Air Classrooms," *Science and Children*, 7:7, March 1970.

Mitchell, John G. "The Bitter Struggle for a National Park," *American Heritage*, 31:97–109, April 1970.

Mueller, Marti, "Everglades Jetport: Academy Prepares a Model," *Science*, 166:202–203, October 10, 1969.

Oberle, Mark. "Endangered Species: Congress Curbs International Trade in Rare Animals," *Science*, 168:152–154, January 9, 1970.

Ott, George. "Is the Bald Eagle Doomed?" *National Wildlife*, 8:4–9, April 1970.

Passer, Jerry E. "A Regional Approach to Conservation Education," *Conservationist*, 24:8–9, June 1970.

Phillips, James. "A Whooping Crane," *Saturday Review*, 53:40, October 3, 1970.

"Rare and Endangered Fish and Wildlife of the United States," *U.S. Bureau of Sport Fisheries and Wildlife Resource Publication* 34. Washington, D.C.: Government Printing Office, 1968.

School Site Development for Conservation and Outdoor Education. Harrisburg: Pennsylvania Department of Education, 1969.

"The Space Available," *Environment*, 12:2–9, March 1970.

Stegner, Wallace. "Conservation Equals Survival," *American Heritage*, 21:114–117, August 1970.

Sullivan, Walter. "Our Last Great Wilderness: Trans-Alaska Pipeline System or TAPS," *American Heritage*, 21:114–117, August 1970.

Swatek, Paul. *The User's Guide to the Protection of the Environment.* New York: Ballatine, 1970.

Talbot, Lee M. "Endangered Species," *Bioscience*, 20:331, March 1970.

Teal, John & Mildred Teal. *Life and Death of the Salt Marsh.* Boston: Little, Brown, 1969.

Udall, Stewart. *1976: Agenda for Tomorrow.* New York: Harcourt, 1968.

Udall, Stewart. *The Quiet Crisis.* New York: Holt, 1963.

Williams, Greer. *The Plague Killers.* New York: Scribner's, 1969.

Zurhorst, Charles. *The Conservation Fraud.* New York: Cowles, 1970.

chapter 7 / population, food, and health

POPULATION

All the problems of air, water, soil, and sound pollution; all the types of pollutants; and all the shortages of resources on the planet earth can be traced to one single source—man. Any attempts to deal with pollution and to resolve critical shortages of resources require man to control his own numbers. Accumulating information reveals the inevitability of widespread starvation in the next ten to fifteen years unless drastic steps are taken to arrest the present rate of population growth.

Although the rate of population increase is much more rapid in developing countries like India, Pakistan, the Philippines, Honduras, Haiti, and the new African nations, increases in highly developed nations cause much heavier drains on resources and much greater pollution rates. Cousins has pointed out that, in terms of environmental pollution, the United States is one of the most overpopulated countries in the world. The average American uses as much eletcric power as do fifty-five Asians and Africans and puts as much carbon monoxide into the air as do 200 residents of Pakistan and India. Indonesia is cited as a prime example of overcrowding, yet a single American puts more pesticides, radioactive substances, fertilizers, and fungicides into the rivers and oceans than do 1,000 people in Indonesia (Cousins, 1970).

Concomitant with an examination of population and its changing patterns on the earth is the necessity to look at food requirements and means of producing and distributing food to the hungry peoples of the world. Nutrition and human health, as well as abuses like using drugs, smoking, overeating, unbalanced diet, and failure to exercise physical and mental powers involve human relations with the environment that will be examined in this chapter.

World Population, 1970

The current rate of population growth throughout the world is 2 percent a year. This rate will double the world's population in thirty-five years. Population growth can be compared to the growth of money invested in a bank at compound interest. Not only are there more people, but these people also multiply at the same rate. Without such compounding it would take fifty years to double the population at a rate of 2 percent. If we look at the times required to double world population in the past we achieve a clearer grasp of the rapidity of population growth today. Between the beginning of recorded history and A.D. 1650 the world's population reached 500 million; by 1850 it had reached 1 billion; by 1930 the figure stood at 2 billion. In mid-1969 the world's population was 3.35 billion (see Table 7.1).

Far more important is the rate of increase in particular countries. Although the present doubling time is thirty-five years for the whole world, it is much shorter for some countries (see Table 7.2).

Table 7.2 shows that the countries of Latin America and Southeast Asia are increasing their populations at the most rapid rates. Those countries that are unable to supply their own needs and have not advanced as rapidly in technology and science as have developed countries generally have the most rapid population growth.

Density

Distribution of people over the surface of the earth is a prime limiting factor in continued population growth. Although any traveler through the desert and mountain regions of the western United States can attest to vast areas of sparsely populated land, there are very overcrowded conditions in New York City, Chicago, and Los Angeles. Ehrlich and Ehrlich (1970) has crudely estimated the population per square mile in various parts of this country in the 1960s. The average density in the United States was fifty-five people per square mile; in New York City it was 25,000 and in Manhattan

Table 7.1. Doubling Times for World Population

Date	Estimated World Population	Doubling Time
1650	500 million	
1850	1 billion	200 years
1930	2 billion	80 years
1975 (projected)	4 billion	45 years

Table 7.2. Estimated Doubling Times for Populations in Some Countries

Country	Population in 1970	Estimated Doubling Time (in Years)
Kuwait	700,000	9
Costa Rica	1,800,000	19
Mexico	50,700,000	21
Honduras	2,700,000	21
El Salvador	3,400,000	21
Colombia	21,400,000	21
Ecuador	6,100,000	21
Philippines	38,100,000	21
Pakistan	136,900,000	21
Iran	28,400,000	24
Libya	1,900,000	23
United Arab Republic	33,900,000	25
India	554,600,000	27
Japan	103,500,000	63
United States	205,200,000	70
France	51,100,000	88
Ireland	3,000,000	100
West Germany	58,600,000	117
Belgium	9,700,000	175

Source: 1970 Population Data Sheet, Population Reference Bureau.

an astronomical 75,000. The tendency to concentrate in cities is one problem that government and society must cope with in curbing the population explosion. Java has an estimated 80 million people crammed into the island at a density of 500 people per square mile.

Nearly one-quarter of the world's population was living in cities with 20,000 or more inhabitants in 1960, a 35 percent increase in urban population within a single decade. The trend continues. Urban populations are increasing more rapidly than is the overall world population. There are at least eighty cities in the world with more than 1 million inhabitants each. Tokyo, New York, Shanghai, Moscow, Bombay, Peking, Chicago, Cairo, Rio de Janeiro, Tientsin, Leningrad, Osaka, London, São Paulo, and Mexico City are the largest.

Malthusian Theory

Thomas Malthus, an English clergyman published his *Essay on the Principle of Population* in 1798. He developed the idea that one great impediment to the progress of mankind toward an improved society is the constant tendency of all animated life to increase beyond the nourishment prepared for it. The tendency of every species, including the human species, is, if unchecked, to double once every generation. That is, species increase at geometric rates, whereas under the most favorable circumstances usually found, food production increases only at an arithmetical rate. According to Malthus, without war, pestilence, famine, and other excesses, the human population would increase in the ratios 1:2:4:8:16:32:64:128:256, whereas food increases in the ratios 1:2:3:4:5:6:7:8:9:10. Shortage of food becomes the ultimate check on population growth, though it is not an immediate one except during actual famine. A large proportion of mankind must therefore suffer hunger and malnutrition. An alternative to this plight is for man himself to regulate population growth (Malthus, 1872)

Population increase is brought about by two conditions: a reduction in death rates and an increase in birth rates. In this century dramatic progress has been made in overcoming infectious diseases like malaria, cholera, smallpox, yellow fever, and poliomyelitis; death rates have thus been dramatically reduced.

Rates of population growth are expressed as birth rate minus death rate per 1,000 people. In the 1969 Data Sheet of the Population Reference Bureau the world birth rate per 1,000 population was estimated at 34, the death rate per 1,000 at 15. The rate of population growth was thus 34 − 15, or 19, per 1,000, which is 1.9 percent.

Malthus argued that, when population is allowed to increase unchecked, food production cannot keep pace. He suggested that pestilence, misery, and vice result. We can apply this postulate to a hypothetical population of 1 million people. A generation (twenty-five years) later this figure will double. In another generation it will have doubled again, to 4 million. If adequate food is being produced for the 1 million, then only by the boldest stretch of the imagination can we envision doubling that production in twenty-five years. We would have to use twice as much land, fertilizer, and water, or increase productivity. But in twenty-five years more food for an additional 2 million people would have to be available. If land and other resources could yield only enough food for an additional 1 million people, then famine, hunger, disease, extreme deprivation, and early death would become common. Wars, hurricanes, typhoons, volcanoes, and other natural calamities also serve to check population growth.

Animals Other than Man

Calhoun (1962) has studied the behavior of Norway rats in confinement with abundant food and nesting places and minimum predation and disease. The animals' behavior toward one another revealed a tendency that might limit their increase in numbers. After twenty-seven months the population had become stabilized at 150 adults. Yet adult mortality was so low that 5,000 adults might have been expected from the observed reproduction rate. Infant mortality kept the population from exploding in this way. Stress from social interaction in crowded conditions led to such interruption of maternal behavior that few young rats survived. Calhoun drew the obvious conclusion that the typical behavior of this animal breaks down under the pressures of population density. It is not wise simply to assume that the human species responds similarly, but we should recognize that overcrowding and abnormal living conditions do modify human behavior patterns.

Wynne-Edwards (1964) has described various devices by which most animals hold their populations at fairly steady levels. Given plenty of opportunity for procreation and a low death rate the human population now shows a tendency to expand without limit. He is almost alone in showing this steady upward trend in numbers. It is generally assumed that animals will reproduce young as fast as they can and that the main factors keeping population density within fixed limits are predation, starvation, accidents, and disease. Although this assumption seems reasonable, animals other than man seem, as we have noted in Norway rats, to have systems that ensure certain average densities.

Ardrey (1966) has described how territorial controls regulate the births of new animals. The animal that controls a territory takes the food and exercises the breeding rights. Others may remain in reserve outside the territory, ready for breeding if needed. By this indirect means the group correlates its population and its food supply. Many of man's basic conflicts have centered on territorial rights. One of the reasons for Japan's territorial expansion to the Asian mainland was its high population density. When World War II ended, the Japanese government began to institute population controls so that the nation could live in the limited space on the islands of Japan.

The Myth of the Lemmings

The lemming has often been cited as a species that commits mass suicide when population increases exceed potential food supplies. This story appears to be a fable, which perhaps owes its longevity to its romantic simplicity. In recent years scientific information on this animal's behavior has destroyed the myth. The lemming is a rodent that lives in Arctic tundras in northern Europe and North America. It is found abundantly in Scandinavia, Alaska, Greenland, Canada, and sometimes the northern United States. It multiplies rapidly, and when its food is scarce its numbers dwindle. Several theories have been advanced to explain the erratic population cycles of this enigmatic animal. Some researchers believe that overcrowding can cause hormone changes that result in a form of birth control.

Mullen and Quay (1969) have isolated a substance in lemming blood that they believe acts as an antifreeze, protecting the animals through Arctic winters and allowing them to remain active instead of hibernating. Supposedly, higher temperatures convert this substance into toxic material that attacks the central nervous system, killing most of the population.

Clough (1965) studied the behavior of Norwegian lemmings in 1963 and 1964, in hopes of learning new information about this species that might have bearing on the problems of human population increase and rapid technological development. Lemming populations do fluctuate drastically from time to time, and occasionally the animals move considerable distances from their original homes. Clough's study produced no information beyond what was already known, but he did make inferences that may ultimately be relevant to human population problems. This animal's population rate varies according to environmental conditions, an adaptation that man will also have to learn to make. The interdependence of all living creatures has been well documented in studies of lemming behavior. Appreciation of this fact is necessary to guide man in his behavior toward other organisms in his ecosystem. Man is only part of a whole natural system. He is powerful within the system, but he is nonetheless dependent upon it.

FOOD

Because world population is growing at an annual rate of approximately 2 percent, food production must increase at a corresponding rate in order even to maintain present levels of nourishment. Such an increase must be sought until population controls can take effect, or human misery will continue rampant in many parts of the earth. Man must decide what he cherishes most. The famous historian Arnold Toynbee raised the basic philosophical question before a conference of the Food and Agriculture Organization of the United Nations in Rome in 1959:

> What is the true end of Man? Is it to populate the Earth with the maximum number of human beings that can be kept alive simultaneously by the world's maximum food supply? Or is it to enable human beings to lead the best kind of life that the spiritual limitations of human nature allow? The first of these two possible objectives seems irrational. What matters, surely, is not that the surface of this planet should hold say, four thousand million instead of three thousand million human beings; what matters is that living beings, whatever their number, shall develop the highest capacities of their nature; and, if this is the true end of Man, what we should aim at is the optimum size of population for this purpose in the economic and social circumstances of each successive generation. (Toynbee, 1966)

Human Nutrition

While mankind was trying to find ways to produce sufficient food for 3.35 billion people in 1970 and the predicted increase in the future, the problem of protein malnutrition is becoming increasingly severe in many developing nations. An adequate diet provides calories to meet the energy needs of the body, proteins to serve as building material, and vitamins and minerals. Energy is provided principally by carbohydrates (starches and sugars) and fats (lipids). The four basic food groups in a nutritionally balanced diet supply adequate amounts of protein for building and repair of body tissues, carbohydrates and fats for energy, and vitamins and minerals to keep the body healthy and help ward off infection.

The calorie is a unit of heat energy and the common measure of the energy provided by certain quantities of specific food substances. Comparison of national food consumption data has shown that much of the population of Asia, Central America, parts of South America, Africa, and the Caribbean exist on fewer than 2,360 calories a day per person; the recommended amount for an average adult. In the United States the average adult consumes 3,200 calories a day. Although minimum calorie requirements suggest how much food is necessary for energy, they imply nothing about vitamins and minerals or the balance of carbohydrates, fats, and proteins necessary for a nutritious diet (*The World Food Budget*, 1964, p. 25).

Attempts to resolve food shortages have traditionally centered on rice, wheat, and corn production. Rice is the staple food of one-third of the world's people. Seven thousand varieties are grown in a band from the equator to Czechoslovakia and Hungary. Mainland China, India, Pakistan, Japan, Indonesia, and countries in Southeast Asia depend heavily upon this cereal grain for their main food. Peoples of Central and South America are corn eaters, whereas wheat is the cereal grain of northern India, parts of Africa, and the Arab countries.

Dependence upon these three cereal grains as the principal source of food leads to protein deficiencies. Both livestock and men must have at least 12 percent of their calorie intake in the form of proteins. Plant protein is not immediately digestible as animal protein is; therefore man is advised to consume something more than his minimum requirement of protein, perhaps 15 percent of his calorie intake. Development of new high-yield rice and wheat strains has been a major accomplishment in fulfilling world food needs, but the protein content is even lower in these new varieties. High-yield rice is only 5–7 percent protein, high-yield wheat is 10 percent protein, and hybrid corn is 7 percent protein. A person subsisting on one of these grains and receiving sufficient calories would still be receiving less than the minimum 12 percent protein requirement. In trying to fill hungry bellies with more calories, man may thus jeopardize his whole defense system through insufficient protein for building and restoring body tissues (Borgstrom, 1969).

Malnourishment, a condition in which food supplies enough or even more energy than the body is using but is deficient in some essential nutrient, is estimated to afflict 60 percent of the people in underdeveloped countries.

Protein is the most common deficiency. Marasmus, a "protein-calorie deficiency," probably results from overall undernourishment. Kwashiorkor is a disease caused by protein deficiency; in West Africa babies develop it when weaned, often after the births of other children. The weanling is usually put on a carbohydrate diet lacking essential nutrients to provide adequate amounts of the twenty amino acids essential to manufacture of body protein. The body can synthesize ten of the twenty but must obtain the remaining ten directly from food. In 1969 people the world over were horrified by pictures of Ibo children, victims of the Biafran civil war in Nigeria, who were dying from kwashiorkor. Swollen limbs, skin sores, bloated bellies, discolored hair, and apathy are all characteristics of children suffering this protein deficiency.

Protein Malnourishment and Intellectual Development

A great deal of evidence that protein deficiency during the period of rapid neurological growth causes irreversible damage to the intellectual development of a child has been gathered in recent years. During the prenatal stages and in the first three or four years of life the brain and nervous system undergo an extraordinarily rapid growth in proportion to other body organs and tissues. The brain doubles in weight during the first six months of a baby's life, and this weight doubles again before he is two years old. Bakan (1970) has cited several research studies of human beings that confirm earlier findings among rats and pigs. Undernourishment results in specific degeneration within brain cells; the earlier the restriction occurs, the more severe the damage is. Of course, human brain cells cannot be measured and weighed as can those of animals. An indirect measure that is widely employed is the rate of increase in head circumference. Performance of children on psychological tests is also related to nutritional factors; the greatest deficit revealed in some studies was in language development.

Elementary-school teachers must be aware of the importance of proper nourishment to the growing child's learning ability. One of the first effects of malnourishment is lack of interest and developing apathy. The child simply does not respond to stimulation with alertness. If his physical requirements are not being met, a teacher is wasting valuable time trying to make him learn. The teacher can investigate the child's eating habits and refer him for help to the proper authority, whether it be the school nurse, guidance counselor, or psychologist.

Increasing Protein in the Diet

The most efficient sources of the ten amino acids that we cannot synthesize are animal proteins. In the United States beef, pork, poultry, and fish are available to fill this need. In Japan and many Southeast Asian countries fish is the principal source of animal protein. Various approaches to increasing the protein content of human diets are being tested. Some familiar sources of protein are plants. Legumes, soybeans and peanuts, pulses (chickpeas, cowpeas, lentils, mung beans, and pigeon peas) have two or three times the protein content of the grasses and are important in supplying essential amino acids. Pulses are 20–25 percent protein and have been a cheap, readily available food since biblical times. Although the pulses contain all ten amino acids, the proportions are not ideal for the human body.

The importance of legumes hinges upon the ability of bacteria in their root nodules to convert atmospheric nitrogen into nitrates usable by plants. Man needs these plants to feed domesticated animals, which convert them into high-quality protein that can be digested by human beings. Amino acids from peanuts, soybeans, and pulses can be consumed directly by human beings.

Protein supplements have been manufactured to supplement the cereal grains. As many people in the developing countries have strong cultural and religious traditions related to food, the protein must come in a form acceptable to them. A product called Incaparina, containing corn-meal enriched with cottonseed meal (which is high in protein), yeast powder, and vitamins has been widely accepted in Central and South America, where the basic diet has always been some form of corn.

Ways are being found to divert soybeans from livestock feed into human food, saving the energy loss incurred by going through a primary consumer before man uses the protein. Soybeans yield about 50 percent more edible protein per acre than does wheat. Alfalfa yields five times more edible protein than does wheat. Ways must be found to market a palatable concentrated alfalfa food for human use.

Water plants, from one-celled algae to giant sea kelp, offer potentially high yields of edible protein per acre. Microorganisms that might first be used as animal feed and later developed as food for human beings are another source of protein. Cellulose wastes—leaves, corncobs, sugarcane pulp, and wood and paper-mill wastes—can be converted into high-protein feeds by microorganisms. The concept of recycling can be applied to many waste products that are currently liabilities to many industries.

Relevance to the Elementary-School Curriculum

Population and food production are global problems today; therefore instilling understanding of these problems is a responsibility of the schools. Environmental awareness includes a conscience for the deprived people of the world. Children must become conscious of the problems of population, birth control and family planning, and human nutrition. They need to understand how governments can exert influence in solving these problems.

Elementary schools have long included personal hygiene and health in their programs. More emphasis should be placed on the health consequences of improper diet, including insufficient amino acids, too much starch and sugar and overconsumption of saturated fats, particularly animal fats. Children should learn to eat vegetable protein from sources like lentils, pulses, and different varieties of beans. They must develop appetites for poultry and fish, as well as for beef and pork.

They must learn that there is no magic pill that will help an overweight person to reduce. Only a caloric intake lower than daily energy needs will be effective. Teachers must set examples in eating and health habits. Knowledge, understanding, and appropriate behavior changes are all required.

HEALTH

Changing Disease Patterns

Until the second half of the twentieth century the health professions were preoccupied with the infectious and biological causes of disease; little attention was paid to physical and chemical aspects caused by environmental pollution. Development of vaccines and antibiotics, along with improved living standards, has sharply reduced the frequency of malaria, tuberculosis, diphtheria, smallpox, yellow fever, and poliomyelitis as major causes of death. Changes in disease patterns, in which infectious diseases have been replaced by killers like heart disease, high blood pressure and stroke, cancer (particularly lung cancer), and chronic bronchitis and emphysema as major causes of death have led physicians to search for physical and chemical roots in the environment.

An alarming increase in deaths from diseases of the heart and blood vessels is discernible. Although these ailments were responsible for 20 percent of the deaths in the United States in the early 1900s, more than half of the deaths in 1962 could be attributed to some type of heart disease. In 1967, 31 percent of the 1,833,900 deaths in this country were traced to such causes ("The Health Consequences of Smoking, 1968 Supplement," p. 16).

Lung cancer, a rarity in 1940, has become the most common cause of cancer deaths among American males. There were 48,000 such deaths in 1967, and it was expected that there would be 51,000 in 1970. This figure is thirteen times higher than it was in 1935. The incidence of emphysema, accompanied by bronchitis or not, has doubled every five years since 1945. All these diseases have risen to almost epidemic proportions in the last twenty-five years (Carnow, 1970). Nine out of every ten lung-cancer victims are smokers.

Smoking, Diet, and Heart Disease

The American Heart Association, with funds from the U.S. Department of Health, Education, and Welfare, recently released a study of heart disease in human beings. It reported that diet, smoking, and work and relaxation habits all contribute to heart disease. People whose diets include high proportions of cholesterol are more likely to develop arteriosclerosis, a thickening of the arteries through deposits of fatty materials. Smoking, high blood pressure, and high fat content in the blood raise the risk that a man will suffer a heart attack. This study was conducted by 115 health experts in 22 countries. People who eat a lot of fat meat and butter, which have higher proportions of saturated fats than do vegetable sources, are more likely to have heart trouble. A direct relationship between cigarette smoking and heart disease was also noted. The earlier that a person starts to smoke and the more heavily that he smokes, the more likely he is to have heart trouble. Overweight, insufficient exercise, and tension in work and other activities all increase the risk of heart disease ("The Good Life Versus Your Heart," 1970).

The implications of this study and available information on emphysema and bronchial disease indicate the urgency of changing the smoking and eating habits of the American people. Children must grow up knowing the consequences of smoking and the health hazards in improper diet and inadequate exercise.

Smoking and Health, the report of the Advisory Committee to the Surgeon General of the Public Health Service published in 1964, first called public attention to the major health hazard created by cigarette smoking. It emphasized, first, that cigarette smoking far outweighs all other causes of lung cancer in men; second, that it is the most important cause of chronic bronchitis in the United States and increases the risk of death from that disease and from emphysema, and, third, that male cigarette smokers have a higher death rate from coronary disease than do nonsmokers (Advisory Committee to the Surgeon General, 1964). In 1967 the Public Health Service reviewed the research literature that had appeared since 1964 (U.S. Public Health Service, 1967); supplemental reports were issued in 1968 and 1969 (U.S. Public Health Service, 1968, 1969). The 1969 supplement provided new evidence linking cigarette smoking with coronary disease, chronic bronchitis, pulmonary emphysema, throat and respiratory cancer, and—for the first time—noncancerous diseases of the mouth. It also cited data suggesting that women who smoke during pregnancy increase the risk of spontaneous abortion, endanger their unborn fetuses, and precipitate premature births.

Air Pollution, Cigarette Smoking, and Lung Cancer

Air pollution has been suspected as a cause of lung cancer, especially because workers in certain high-pollution industries are more likely to suffer lung disorders. Byssinosis, which scars and destroys the lungs of cotton workers, silicosis in foundry workers, and pneumoconiosis in coal miners are all caused by inhalation of large concentrations of particles. Lung cancer is abnormally frequent among workers exposed to uranium, nickel, chromates, and asbestos. An asbestos worker who smokes has ninety times as high a chance of developing lung cancer as does a nonsmoker who works in unpolluted conditions.

The May 1970 issue of *UNESCO Courier* is devoted to cancer and what can be and is being done about it. In this publication Waller has cited several studies conducted in Germany, the United States, and Great Britain that have revealed clear connections between cigarette smoking and lung cancer. It has been established that deaths from lung cancer increase among people who live where the air is heavily polluted with benzo(a)-pyrene, a product of coal burning. Although in very polluted areas death rates are higher for both nonsmokers and for most smokers, smoking is still the major factor in determining the rates.

The increase in cigarette use that began in the 1920s first manifested itself in deaths from lung cancer about twenty years later. It takes a long time to produce a cancer, and it is this fact that makes it so difficult to convince people that smoking is dangerous. They cannot see immediate damage to their systems and are less concerned about their health twenty years from now than about their social popularity today.

Some people claim that it has not been proved that smoking causes cancer. But Nikolai Blokhin, President of the International Union Against Cancer, has replied: "Tobacco is not a direct cause of lung cancer, but the habit of smoking contributes to the development of precancerous conditions and subsequently of malignant tumors. Cigarettes are also an aggravating factor in cardiovascular illnesses, which are the commonest cause of death in a great many countries" (Godber, 1970, p. 11).

Some countries have recognized their governments' responsibilities to their citizens in this matter. In Italy all cigarette advertising has been stopped. In Norway showing smoking on television has been materially reduced. In the United States cigarette advertising on television was banned on January 1, 1971. Restrictions on cigarette advertising are also in force in Czechoslovakia, Denmark, France, Ireland, Norway, Sweden, and Switzerland.

Implications for the Elementary School

The evidence is clear. All available scientific studies point to the increased likelihood that smokers will develop heart disease or lung cancer, the two leading causes of death in the country today. The school can no longer leave out of its curriculum teaching about smoking and health. It is just as important to develop understanding of the consequences to health of smoking as it is to learn to brush teeth, wash hands, and drink plenty of milk.

The most effective way in which schools can teach is by example. It is futile to talk about the harmful effects of smoking in the classroom if a child cannot see across the teachers' lounge because of the smoky air. Children do emulate their models. The elementary school is one place where the model is usually an adult. In high school peers become models, and teachers' examples will have little impact in many instances.

Drug use has become a serious problem among the young people of our nation. There are "pickup" drugs and "slowdown" drugs. From aspirin for headaches to heroin for addicts we rely on an endless variety of chemical resolutions for all discomforts and problems of life. Unfortunately, the problems do not go away, and drugs do not make life more satisfying.

The inclusion of information on drug use and abuse in environmental education at the elementary level is necessary because children today are often exposed to pushers at an early age. Some children as young as ten or twelve years old already use marihuana and "hard" drugs.

The first step in dealing with drug problems is to know what the drugs are. Many publications on both legitimate and prohibited drugs are available. Teachers must inform themselves of the types of drugs to which children may be exposed and of how drug users can be identified. *A Guide to Some Drugs Which Are Subject to Abuse* (1970), published by the American Social Health Association, describes hallucinogens, heroin, and marihuana, as well as drugs manufactured and distributed through ethical channels. Some questions about drugs are answered in Public Health Service publications nos. 1828 (on LSD), 1829 (on marihuana), and 1830 (on the amphetamines and barbiturates). These publications are generally available through local health departments.

Children are likely to seek their first drug thrills through breathing the vapors of model-airplane glue. Irritability, inattentiveness, and drowsiness, as well as signs of physical sickness, are symptoms that might cause teachers to suspect glue sniffing or use of amphetamines or barbiturates.

Loss of emotional control and social and intellectual breakdown are general consequences of all drugs taken in excess.

Much discussion of possible legalization of marihuana has arisen. But no medical authority has yet presented evidence of beneficial effects from its use. Marihuana use can be the first step to heroin or other "hard" drugs. Society cannot therefore remove legal restrictions upon its sale and possession without expecting to reap a crop of new "hard" drug users. Regardless of arguments for legalization, possession and use of marihuana are illegal, and the penalties for violations are harsh. Conviction for possession can lead to imprisonment for two to ten years and fines up to $20,000.

LSD (often called "acid") and other hallucinogens are reputed to have "mind expanding" properties. An average dose, amounting to a speck, is often taken in a sugar cube, cracker, or cookie, or it can be licked off a stamp coated with the drug. Of course, children are easily tempted by gifts of candy or food that may contain drugs. Some of the most frightening effects of these drugs may be recurrent "flashbacks" many months after the drug has been taken, which can lead to depression and suicide. Recent evidence also indicates that LSD may damage chromosomes, which could lead to birth defects.

Learning about the characteristics of drugs—how to spot them and their users, effects upon users, and slang names—is fundamental to an environmentally aware person. How can children be taught the dangers of drugs in such a way that they will avoid victimization by this lurking menace? Certainly more than intellectual appeal is necessary. They must have the facts, but they must also have teachers who are understanding and attentive to their problems. Children are certainly more influenced by emotions than by reason. Those who find satisfaction in other ways are less likely to seek chemical means of escape from the stresses to which contemporary life subjects them.

INVESTIGATIONS

1. Make a picture of a crowded city and one of a rural area. What pollution problems are different in the two areas? What are the differences in demand for resources in these two areas?

2. Investigate various populations: of the school, family, city, county, and state. Find out how such information is obtained and what uses are made of it. Prepare a map showing population densities, shading areas of different densities in different colors.

3. Observe the results of overpopulation among goldfish. Fill two aquariums of widely different sizes—perhaps a quart jar and a ten-gallon

tank—with water that has stood for twenty-four hours to adjust it to room temperature and evaporate the chlorine. Put four healthy, medium-sized goldfish in each. Pupils can observe and record different reactions to the two environments. Encourage them to keep any important daily observations in notebooks. The two aquariums should be kept in the room for a month or more. Let the pupils try to predict changes in the goldfish population.

Investigations of goldfish can be expanded to include other variables: plant life, food, snails, and pH of the water. Students should be encouraged to think up their own investigations. They may find ideas in Breder's experiments with guppies (1932), as well as in the studies of Norway rats and lemmings described in this chapter.

4. What causes changes in populations of yeast cells? This question is excellent for a pupil interested in a special project. Many fourth-, fifth-, and sixth-graders have their own microscopes and would be fascinated by this inquiry.

   Place about fifteen granules of dry yeast in a 250-milliliter beaker containing 100 milliliters of sterile water. Stir until the yeast is evenly suspended in the water, and then examine a drop under the microscope (at 100× magnification). Count the number of yeast cells in several different fields; then average them.

   Divide the yeast solution equally among ten test tubes. Plug with cotton, and place nine in the refrigerator. Store the other tube at room temperature after adding a half-gram of sugar. This tube should be labeled "Number 1" and dated.

   On each successive day remove one test tube from the refrigerator, add a half-gram of sugar, and label it with number, date, and time. Store at room temperature. At the end of ten days, examine (under 100× magnification) a sample drop from each test tube. Be sure to stir the solution before sampling. Count the cells in each field. Count the populations in three or more samples from each tube in order to obtain an average for the whole tube. Record the results in tabular form. Plot the results on a graph, correlating days of growth and average numbers of cells.

   What is the limiting factor in growth of yeast cells? What variations of this investigation are possible? (Different temperatures, different amounts of yeast, different amounts of water, and different initial concentrations of yeast cells can all be tested.)

5. Observation of an ant colony yields insights into how one species lives and relates in a community. A screw-top jar or a house made from two window panes (see figure 7.1) can be used (Hone *et al.*, 1962). Pupils look for kinds of behavior, especially wing growth, which

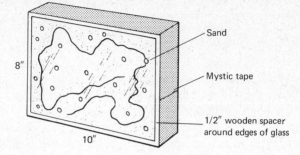

Figure 7.1 Window pane ant house.

occurs only when the colony has reached a certain size and mating takes place. The females then start a new colony.

6. Obtain population figures for your city and state from the U.S. Census counts of several decades. Population growth in the United States occurs at a rate of 1 percent, doubling every seventy years. How does the rate in your city or state compare with the national rate? Consider some of the principal polluters in your community: automobiles, factories, commercial establishments, and so on. Calculate how many more of them will be added to the environment if they keep pace with population increases. How many more cars can you expect if the population doubles in your city? Where will they go? How much more land will be paved and lost to natural plant and animal habitation?

7. Some supermarket chains have begun to label a variety of food products with nutritional information. One labeling method names the nutrients present and tells what percentage of the recommended daily allowance of each is represented. Pupils should try to keep records of all the foods consumed by them for one week and examine them to see if they are labeled. Find out from the labeled information whether or not the four basic food groups are included and how much protein is contained in the diet each day. Look for those foods that are high in protein and low in calories. Are the diets of your pupils too high in calories without sufficient protein? Does each child's daily diet include the minimum protein recommendation according to his age and sex? Food nutrient charts can be found in most health books or cookbooks.

8. Are the protein foods that you eat primarily beef and pork, which are likely to be high in saturated fats? If so, find other protein sources that are lower in saturated fats: fish and poultry, beans, pulses, and peanut products. Children should ask their mothers to help find out

how much fat is in the hamburger, bacon, or pork chops that they eat. Can some of that fat be eliminated? Why?

9. Keep a record of the school cafeteria lunches for a week, calculating the calories per serving and the percentage that is protein. Find out from the cafeteria manager how she plans the menus. Perhaps you can suggest your preferences to her after she tells you what food supplies are available.

10. Investigate the effects on you of an unbalanced diet. Describe diseases and bodily dysfunctions that may occur if you do not receive sufficient protein, vitamins, minerals, calories, carbohydrates, and fats.

11. Clip newspapers and magazines for articles and pictures showing hungry children around the world. Become more conscious of our privileges in having plenty of wholesome food, including fresh fruits and vegetables. But also study the facts about hunger in this country from works like Harrington's *The Other America* (1963).

12. What do you think it means to say that many overweight Americans are overfed and undernourished? How should eating habits be changed to correct such conditions? Nutrition experts say that many Americans are eating themselves to death. Income level does not necessarily determine the quality of diet. Why?

13. Children should learn to eat some foods that they do not customarily eat: perhaps broccoli, spinach, or other leafy greens that are rich in the vitamins and iron that many people chronically lack.

14. Find out about how long vegetables should be cooked for maximum nutritional value and vitamins. Vitamins C and D are water-soluble, and vitamins A and D are fat-soluble. Which vitamins can be boiled away?

15. *Smoking and Health Experiments, Demonstrations, and Exhibits* (U.S. Department of Health, Education, and Welfare, 1969) is the best source of information on the subject for teachers. It describes twenty or more ways in which cigarette smoke can be investigated through effects on living things and on the human body. A simple cigarette-smoking apparatus can be assembled from a gallon jar with a two-hole stopper, delivery tubes, and a suction pump. The kind of suction bulb used to fill batteries in service stations makes a satisfactory suction pump. Assemble the apparatus, fill the jar half full of water, put a cigarette in the "intake," and light it. Draw smoke through the jar of water until the cigarette is about half smoked. What changes do you note in the water, in the air above the water, and in the tubes?

After removing the stopper hold your hand over the opening, and shake the water in the jar. What changes do you note in the water? What smell is prevalent? What effect do you think twenty cigarettes a day might have on a person's lungs if the changes noted are caused by only one cigarette?

16. Place a small fish in the water from investigation 15. As soon as it appears to have been affected by the poison, place it in freshly aerated water to revive. If nicotine poisoning can affect a fish so quickly, imagine how a person might ultimately be affected by continued smoking.

17. The senses of taste and smell are usually weakened in smokers, because of the numbing effects of tobacco on nerve endings in the nose and throat. The effects can be compared with those of extreme cold. Apply an ice cube to the tongue of a pupil, and test his ability to taste sweet, sour, bitter, and salty substances.

18. Local chapters of the Tuberculosis and Respiratory Disease Association are anxious to spread information about the effects of smoking and air pollution on human health. A cross section of two diseased lungs can be compared with a cross section of two sound lungs. Also, a doctor, nurse, or medical assistant may come to explain and illustrate the health hazards of smoking.

19. Classroom drug education consists predominantly of gathering accurate knowledge about drugs—the physical effects on users and especially the social and psychological effects. Carpenter (1970) and "Drugs" (1969) offer various useful related activities for grades four through nine. Some people believe that drug education should begin in kindergarten, with activities like this one and the next.

    Ask children what chemicals their mothers use at home and which are kept out of their reach. They may include lye, cleaning fluid, ammonia, detergents. What precautions must be exercised in handling them?

20. Ask the children to name some of the medicines in their home medicine cabinets. Parents must understand the purpose of this activity and, of course, children need not hear about private medication.

21. Clip the abundant magazine and newspaper articles on drug abuse. Keeping such information should become a class project. Some current television advertising is designed to make children of intermediate-school age aware of attempts to steer them to drugs.

22. Children should try to gather information about people who have used drugs and reported beneficial effects.

23. The class might write and produce an advertisement showing advantages of taking drugs as drug pushers describe them, followed by one showing the actual effects of drug use, based on information gathered about users.

24. Study the history of drug development. Consider aspirin, penicillin, laxatives, "liver pills," quinine, and so on.

25. Sixth- and seventh-grade pupils can read books or stories describing unusual circumstances in history related to drugs—for example, *The Day of Saint Anthony's Fire* (Fuller, 1968) tells how ergot in wheat is related to LSD.

26. Prepare charts of legitimate drugs, showing their names, purposes, legal controls, dangers, and symptoms of abuse. List common misconceptions about them. Prepare a similar chart for illicit drugs, including LSD, mescaline, hashish, heroin, and marihuana. Be sure to emphasize the consequences of having, using, or selling any illegal drug.

27. Show one of the available films on drugs.

28. Invite a member of the medical or pharmaceutical profession to talk about the medical consequences of drugs. Someone who can present the facts accurately and objectively without moralizing is more likely to be effective.

29. A former drug user might be an effective speaker to older children. But reformed addicts often have personal problems that make it inadvisable to expose elementary-school children to them. Choose speakers with caution.

30. Compile a glossary of slang expressions used in relation to drugs. It is better to know the words commonly used than to avoid them because they are incorrect English.

31. Describe the emotions fear, joy, happiness, depression, and love. How does a person reach each of these emotional states without using drugs? Can you think of pursuits by which you can achieve each emotional state by other means than drugs?

SPECIAL RESOURCES

Alfred Higgins Productions, 9100 Sunset Boulevard, Los Angeles, California 90069. Film, *Your Amazing Mind*, about drugs, for upper elementary-school children.

Bailey-Film Associates, 11559 Santa Monica Boulevard, Los Angeles, California 90025. Films, *LSD: Insight or Insanity* and *Marijuana.*

Churchill Films, 662 N. Robertson Boulevard, Los Angeles, California 90069. Film, *Drugs and the Nervous System.*

Encyclopaedia Britannica Educational Corp., 425 N. Michigan Avenue, Chicago, Illinois 60611. Filmstrip, "Drug Misuse and Your Health."

Eye Gate House, Inc., 146-01 Archer Avenue, Jamaica, New York 11435. Filmstrips, "Narcotics—Background Information" and "Drugs and Health."

Air Pollution Primer. New York: National Tuberculosis and Respiratory Disease Association, 1969. Pamphlet, especially good for specific facts about the effects of air pollution on human health.

Population and Family Planning Programs: A Factbook. New York: Population Council & International Institute for the Study of Human Reproduction, Columbia University, 1969.

REFERENCES

Abelson, Philip H. "LSD and Marijuana," *Science*, 159:1189, March 15, 1968.

Advisory Committee to the Surgeon General. *Smoking and Health.* Public Health Service Publication No. 1103. Washington, D.C.: Government Printing Office, 1964.

Ardrey, Robert. *The Territorial Imperative.* New York: Atheneum, 1966.

Bakan, Rita. "Malnutrition and Learning," *Phi Delta Kappan*, 51:527–530, June 1970.

Biological Sciences Curriculum Study. *Biological Science: An Inquiry into Life,* 2nd ed. New York: Harcourt, 1968.

Biological Sciences Curriculum Study. *High School Biology: Green Version,* 2nd ed. Chicago: Rand McNally, 1968.

Borgstrom, Georg. *Too Many: A Study of Earth's Biological Limitations.* New York: Macmillan, 1969.

Breder, C. M., Jr., & C. W. Coates. "Population Stability and Sex Ratio of Lebistes." *Copeia*, No. 3, 147–155, October 7, 1932.

Brownell, L. E. "New Approaches to the World Food Problem," *The Science Teacher*, 37:23–25, March 1970.

Browning, T. O. *Animal Populations.* New York: Harper, 1963.

Calhoun, John B. "Population Density and Social Pathology," *Scientific American*, 206:32, 139–146, February 1962.

Carnow, Bertram W. "Pollution Invites Disease," *Saturday Review*, 53:38–40, July 4, 1970.

Carpenter, Regan. "Drug Education: Take Out the Glamor!" *Instructor*, 80:130–133, August 1970.

"Classroom-Tested Techniques for Teaching about Smoking," *NEA Journal*, 56:37–52, December 1967. Also available as a pamphlet from National Clearinghouse for Smoking and Health, U.S. Public Health Service, 4040 North Fairfax Drive, Arlington, Virginia 22203.

Clough, Garrett C. "Lemmings and Population Problems," *American Scientist*, 53:199–212, June 1965.

Cousins, Norman. "Affluence and Effluence," *Saturday Review*, 53:53, May 2, 1970.

"Drugs," *Grade Teacher*, 87:97–102, November 1969.

"Drugs and the Educational Antidote," *Nation's Schools*, 85:49–52, April 1970.

Ehrlich, Paul. *The Population Bomb*. New York: Ballantine, 1968.

Ehrlich, Paul & Anne Ehrlich. *Population, Resources, Environment*. San Francisco: Freeman, 1970.

Fuller, John G. *The Day of St. Anthony's Fire*. New York: Macmillan, 1968.

Garrett, W. E. "Canada's Heartland: The Prairie Provinces," *National Geographic*, 138:443–489, October 1970.

Godber, George. "Cigarettes and Cancer," *UNESCO Courier*, 23:10–13, May 1970.

"The Good Life Versus Your Health," *U.S. News and World Report*, 69:29, December 28, 1970.

A Guide to Some Drugs Which Are Subject to Abuse. New York: American Social Health Association, 1970.

Harrington, Michael. *The Other America: Poverty in the United States*. Baltimore: Penguin, 1963.

Hone, Elizabeth B., Alexander Joseph & Edward Victor. *A Sourcebook for Elementary Science*. New York: Harcourt, 1962.

Jacobs, Lewis. "Human Intelligence—The Physiological View," *The Science Teacher*, 35:13–17, September 1968.

Leach, Glen. "Drug Abuse Is Hitting Younger Children," *Instructor*, 79:60–61, August 1969.

Malthus, T. R. *An Essay on the Principle of Population*, 7th ed. London: Reeves and Turner, 1872.

Mead, Margaret. "The Changing Significance of Food," *American Scientist*, 58:176, March 1970.

Mullen, David & William Quay. "The Mysterious Lemmings," *Chemistry*, 42:3, September 1969.

Myrdal, G. "The World Is Heading for a Collision," *UNESCO Courier*, 19:21–24, February 1966.

Paddock, William & Paul Paddock. *Famine, 1975*. Boston: Little, Brown, 1967.

Petersen, William. *The Politics of Population*. New York: Doubleday, 1964.

Pirie, N. W. "Orthodox and Unorthodox Methods of Meeting World Food Needs," *Scientific American*, 216:27–35, February 1967.

Reitz, Louis P. "New Wheats and Social Progress," *Science*, 169:952–955, September 4, 1970.

Scrimshaw, Nevin S. "Infant Malnutrition and Adult Learning," *Saturday Review*, 51:64–66, March 16, 1968.

Spencer, Steven M. "Marijuana: How Dangerous Is It?" *Reader's Digest*, 99:67–71, January 1970.

Stevero, Richard. "The Horrors of Heroin," *Reader's Digest*, 99:72–75, January 1970.

"Students and Drug Abuse," *Today's Education*, 58:35–50, March 1969.

Swatek, Paul. *The User's Guide to the Protection of the Environment*. New York: Ballantine, 1970.

Toynbee, Arnold. "To Establish an Equilibrium," *UNESCO Courier*, 19:12, February 1966.

U.S. Department of Agriculture. *Food for Us All. 1969 Yearbook of Agriculture*. Washington, D.C.: Government Printing Office, 1969.

U.S. Department of Agriculture, Economic Research Service. *The World Food Budget, 1970. Foreign Agricultural Economics Report No. 19*. Washington, D.C.: Government Printing Office, 1964.

U.S. Department of Health, Education, and Welfare. *Bibliography on Smoking and Health*. Washington, D.C.: Government Printing Office, 1969.

U.S. Department of Health, Education, and Welfare. *Changes in Cigarette Smoking Habits Between 1955 and 1966*. Washington, D.C.: Government Printing Office, 1967.

U.S. Department of Health, Education, and Welfare. "Smoking and Health Experiments, Demonstrations, and Exhibits." *Public Health Service Publication No. 1843*. Washington, D.C.: Government Printing Office, 1969.

U.S. Public Health Service. "The Health Consequences of Smoking: A Public Health Service Review: 1967." *Public Health Service Publication No. 1696*. Washington, D.C.: Government Printing Office, 1967.

U.S. Public Health Service. "The Health Consequences of Smoking: 1968 Supplement." Washington, D.C.: Government Printing Office, 1968.

U.S. Public Health Service. "The Health Consequences of Smoking: 1969 Supplement." Washington, D.C.: Government Printing Office, 1969.

Waller, R. E. "Air Pollution and Lung Cancer," *UNESCO Courier*, 23:30–32, May 1970.

"What You Should Know About the Major Mind-Affecting Drugs," *Good Housekeeping*, 171:148–149, August 1970.

Wynne-Edwards, V. C. "Population Control in Animals," *Scientific American*, 211:68, August 1964.

Yen, Harry S. C. "The Fragile Beauty All About Us," *National Geographic*, 138:785–798, December 1970.

Young, Gordon & James P. Blair. "Pollution: Threat to Man's Own Home," *National Geographic*, 138:738–781, December 1970.

chapter 8/ designing the environment of the future

Glass (1969) has described a situation that arose when a large aluminum-processing plant was built in a Czech valley after World War II. Although some biologists recommended not putting the plant there, their arguments were overriden by stronger considerations. After the plant was in full production, an atmospheric inversion trapped sulfur-dioxide fumes among the hills, killing all plants and driving the animals away. This disaster led to recognition of the need to study the "biological landscape." The Czech experience calls attention to the fact that technological alterations of the natural environment necessitate a new approach to technological assessment. Biological, psychological, and sociocultural, as well as engineering and physicochemical aspects, must be considered in future design.

Man has demonstrated that he can put himself on the moon. He has risen to scientific and technological heights and has achieved phenomenal advances in controlling infectious diseases. But in making life easier for some we have overlooked many who are being smothered in pollution and waste and are being denied the use of the earth's resources.

Biologists and chemists have put together the chemicals necessary to produce life. There is every reason to believe that in the future animal life, even human life itself, will be synthesized from inorganic matter. Frightening though this thought may be, it also inspires hope for what man can do once his resources are appropriately directed.

In the course of history mankind has allowed itself to sink into a morass of pollution, contamination, ugly garbage, debris, and waste in which we now find ourselves. By the same token man alone can design ways to climb out of this morass.

Long-range planning in which every production phase is coordinated with a recycling phase is necessary. We must design cities in which people can live, enjoy the advantages of urbanism, yet maintain a balanced environment. Means of transportation must be developed to move people without contributing vast amounts of the pollutants characteristic of vehicles powered by internal-combustion engines. Aesthetics must become a prime consideration in industry and commerce.

In environmental design not only physical but also human concerns must be important. Health services, care for the aged and deprived, and equal educational opportunities must be incorporated into future environmental design. Such design requires redefinition of national priorities. To become a democratic country, instead of one governed by special interest groups, should be our true goal.

URBAN DESIGN

Most people live in cities. In the United States 70 percent of the population lives on 2 percent of the land. In the 1970 Census there were only slightly more than 10 million farm residents in a total population of more than 200 million. This segment has declined steadily; there were 15 million farm residents in 1960, when the total population was less than 180 million. The movement of people to urban areas has been accompanied by serious social and physical difficulties related to concentration. While the rate of increase in city populations has risen, the quality of life in urban areas has declined. Most of the people who have migrated to cities have been poor, "disadvantaged," and unemployed members of minority groups, including blacks, Puerto Ricans, and Mexican-Americans. At the same time there has been a mass flight of the middle class, of socially dominant and economically affluent members of society, from urban areas to the suburbs or the country. This exchange has resulted in deterioration of social conditions—stealing, destruction of property, loss of respect for others, and generally unacceptable personal behavior—poor housing, increased pupil absenteeism, more dropouts from school, and high levels of unemployment in the inner cities. The rioting that swept Detroit, Newark, Los Angeles, and other cities in the 1960s reflected the unrest and corrosive conditions that prevail in far too many of our cities.

Cities provide physical conditions that do not exist in the country. Concentrations of buildings, pavement, people, and motor vehicles actually produce climatic changes around a city. Temperatures in cities tend to be higher than in the surrounding countryside. In August 1970 the smog accumulation over Tokyo became so heavy that 122 of the city's downtown streets had to be closed to automobiles. In the area within about a twenty-five mile radius of Los Angeles, lettuce cannot be grown. A similar condition exists around Newark, New Jersey, because of air pollution.

A great deal of attention has recently been given to urban design, with consideration of the environmental effects of concentrating great numbers of people. Spilhaus (1969) has defined a city as a system of human services, a place where people have business and social contacts, and a setting for cultural, recreational, and other amenities. He has proposed an experimental city in which services to people are given as much consideration as is housing. Such services would, in an ideal city, be planned to accommodate the population of the city. They include communication, transportation, health, public-utilities, educational, and recreational services. Some of Spilhaus' proposals require emphasis. He has suggested (1967) that no fuel-burning machines be allowed within cities and that connections between city and local transportation systems at a city's periphery be encouraged. The main public utilities could be supplied through tunnels. Utility trenches for transport of heavy freight, telephone lines, power and gas lines, and water and sewer mains could also double as traffic tunnels for emergency vehicles—from the police, the fire, and the ambulance departments. Pneumatic sewers have saved water in some European countries.

The entire idea of a city designed to protect the environment relies heavily on going underground with many of the ugly, noisy, polluting machines and vehicles that currently detract from the pleasantness of cities. Hudson (1970) has described an imaginative space-age city in which vehicular traffic, including a service level with streets for trucks and deliveries, is all below the surface. Mass transportation systems bring people to work, thus permitting walkways with grassy surroundings, small trees, birds, flowers, and small ponds to exist in the remaining space at ground level. In the illustrations accompanying Hudson's article, architectural draughtsman Ralph Winter has envisioned the city designed for coping with modern living. Buildings with terraces where trees and plants can grow, small gardens on roofs where birds are attracted in their migratory paths, and fish ponds on the fiftieth floor are attractions to live and work in such a city. Hudson thinks that use of computerized information storage and retrieval can produce an American city comparable in accomplishment to landing a man on the moon. Architects, engineers, scientists, ecologists, sociologists, city planners, landscape artists, and political leaders must all combine their talents to produce this dream.

TRANSPORTATION

We are a mobile people; 109 million motor vehicles were already on the nation's highways in 1970, and Detroit was predicting a rise to 118–119 million in 1971. Highways, streets, paved areas, interchanges, and other surfaces used by automobiles take up vast amounts of land in this nation. Not only is this land removed from production, but also we lose valuable vegetation necessary to replenish the oxygen supply in the air and to absorb precipitated water, preventing its rapid runoff.

Airplane travel has advanced at a phenomenal rate during the last decade. A person can have breakfast in New York and three hours later have a second breakfast at the same local time in Los Angeles. The Federal government has subsidized airlines, primarily those providing scheduled air service to small communities, where air traffic is not adequate to make the service self-supporting. Development of rapid air travel has made it possible for a person to travel between two airports with greater ease than he can enjoy in traveling from city to airport and the reverse. Airport facilities themselves have not kept pace with aircraft development. Noise levels around airports have produced lawsuits from local residents. Development of still faster aircraft portend even higher noise levels, as well as frequent sonic booms.

Planning for future transportation necessitates more careful consideration of the effects that any type of conveyance will have on the environment. Urban mass transit must be developed to replace private automobiles. We can no longer afford the luxury of letting a six-passenger automobile pollute the air for one or two hours every morning and then take up parking space all day. Stueck (1970) describes the urban-transit system in Hamburg, Germany, which might be taken as a model for many cities of the world. Serving 2.5 million residents in more than 1,000 square miles of territory, this system fulfills functions similar to those needed in many American cities. A subway and an urban train system whose schedules are coordinated with those of suburban bus lines combine to make it possible for a person to commute to his job in less time than an automobile ride would require. Suburban parking lots are available to accommodate autos at bus and train stops. Fewer cars in the inner city mean less atmospheric pollution from motor vehicles. Officials emphasize that relief from pollution by motor exhaust has not meant increased pollution from generation of electricity to run the subways.

Rapid Transit

Rapid trains between cities are also necessary if the number of motor vehicles and the accompanying pollution are to be reduced. The Japanese have a train that travels at speeds up to 130 miles an hour between Tokyo and Osaka. Any traveler to Japan can attest to the dependability and punctuality of the computer-operated train service there. The Metroline train between New York and Washington, D.C., represents an effort in the

United States to cope with rapid transit other than air and auto travel. It averages more than 100 miles an hour and is capable of speeds up to 160 miles an hour; the trip from New York to Washington can be made in less than three hours. The trip by air shuttle requires at least an hour to reach the airport, an hour in flight (if no delays occur), and another hour to reach a destination from the airport at the other end. Tokyo's high-speed monorail from the heart of the city to the airport is another example of the kind of service that would help to relieve automobile congestion and air pollution.

The Highway Trust Fund

The Highway Trust Fund was created by Congress in 1965 to pay for development of the 41,000-mile National Defense Interstate Highway System. More than 5 billion dollars in excise taxes, mostly from the Federal levy of 4 cents a gallon on gasoline, are paid into this fund annually. The fund has poured enormous sums into highways, thus supporting the automobile and trucking industries, but no substantial effort has been made to arouse government support for mass-transit systems. As this law is presently structured, the money collected from automobile use cannot be applied to other types of transportation but must be held in reserve in the Highway Trust Fund. A revision of the law is necessary so that these funds can be used more flexibly.

Supersonic Transport

A supersonic transport plane (SST) capable of traveling at speeds up to 1,800 miles an hour and carrying 273 passengers has been the subject of much debate. In the last weeks of the 91st Congress, conflict over $290 million designated for continued research and development of a prototype SST held up passage of the Transportation Department appropriation. The Federal government proposed to provide financing that might ultimately exceed $1 billion to develop this plane for commercial use. Many arguments have been presented for and against the SST. The principal reasons for it include the need to compete with the British-French Concorde and the Russian TU-144 supersonic planes, the need to provide employment for many people in aircraft and related industries, the need for fast transportation for some people, and the need to keep our nation in the forefront of scientific and technological development. Opposition has centered on the threat of pollution in the stratosphere, which could alter the earth's climate; the use of public money to support a commercial endeavor; uncertainty about the effects of noise and sonic booms on animal and plant life; doubt that such a large expenditure to benefit a relatively small number of people can be justified.

On December 3, 1970, the Senate voted against further appropriation for development of the SST. This defeat of a powerful effort by special-interest groups is a good sign that public opinion on environmental issues is beginning to make itself heard. It was a positive victory resulting from hard work by many concerned environmental groups. An attempt to revive support for the SST in the House was again defeated in the Senate.

AN ENVIRONMENT FOR EDUCATION

Probably an area of our environment that needs as much careful reevaluation as does any other is the environment for learning. Schools suffer sound pollution, children must sit in overheated classrooms, the physical climate is dull, and the emotional and psychological environment lacks the ingredients necessary to stimulate children's interests and motivate them to achieve. Problems of ghetto blight, education of the disadvantaged, and school desegregation have caused educators to seek radically different approaches to education. The children of tomorrow should not be confined in four-walled classrooms when vastly different resources are available to the schools.

Probably the most notable environmental change in school is the tendency to extend the learning environment beyond the bounds of the classroom. Imaginative teachers and administrators are offering many open-air experiences. Holding school in the woods for one week is one approach that gives children a fuller sense of nature. A chance really to observe birds, flowers, plants, trees, insects, stars, rocks, minerals, and wild animals in their natural settings is very valuable, yet classroom subjects like mathematics, language arts, social studies, science, and personal health and hygiene also fit into such a study. One of the most fruitful results of such a week outdoors is the classroom preparations that precede it. Arousing motivation and student interest is not a problem when this project is offered to fifth- or sixth-graders.

Educational parks that more fully integrate the total environment into the school experience are being designed for some cities. Pettigrew (1969) has described a design for a metropolitan educational park on about 100 acres of land, to serve no fewer than fourteen or fifteen schools and kindergarten through twelfth grade. The idea is to locate the park in a suburb or just inside the periphery of the inner city. Such a park could accommodate around 15,000 students at once. Greater use of facilities and services already available within the community must be characteristic of future schools. Children and adolescents should have more access to all resources of their city as part of their education. A manufacturing plant, a newspaper office, city-government offices, a courtroom, a scientific research laboratory, a farm, and a forest can be better places to learn than the classroom is.

RECYCLING MATERIALS

There are finite amounts of most natural resources on earth. Man has always sought to use these resources for his own advantage, and little thought has been given to devising ways to recycle waste materials after use. Recycling permits resources to be used again and also prevents accumulation of solid wastes. About 1 ton of waste is produced by each person in the United States in a year; one-third of it is packaging material. Cans, bottles, and paper containers are the principal solid wastes.

A shredding technique has recently been developed to dispose of wrecked and junked automobiles without the air pollution caused by burning. A machine chops the car into chunks of metal the size of one's hand. Magnets separate ferrous and nonferrous metals, and high-velocity blowers remove upholstery and other nonmetallic matter. This machine is only one example of new means of disposing of wastes and recovering useful material.

Solid sewage can be compressed and used as an agricultural fertilizer or as a soil conditioner for lawns. It is within man's powers to find ways to recycle most of the materials that he uses in his daily life. He could thus produce new materials for use while eliminating much of the pollution that surrounds us.

REORDERING NATIONAL PRIORITIES

In order to "engineer" the future environment and to make it possible for man to realize his full potential in achieving the quality of life that most of us desire, national priorities and goals must be reordered. We can no longer look upon bigger as necessarily better, faster as necessarily most desirable, and production of new machines and gadgets as necessarily beneficial to us individually and collectively. The national budget for 1971 allocated $73 billion for defense and $15 billion for health. When we can spend $3.4 billion for space research and technology and only $2.5 billion for preservation of natural resources, then some values have been misplaced. When the Transportation Department budget has included $290 million for development of a supersonic transport and only $80 million for development of mass transit, then the money is certainly not being spent in the best interests of the most people (U.S. Bureau of the Budget, 1971).

Health Care

Health-care programs should offer services to indigent people in the same degree to which they are available to people who can pay. The shortage of doctors in the United States is a national scandal. Ribicoff (1970) has described a husband who was left with a $30,000 medical bill after his wife's long hospitalization with terminal cancer. This man, a house painter by trade, will never be able to pay this horrendous debt and provide the necessities of life for his four children. Inadequate programs of prevention, as well as lack of manpower, equipment, and facilities, are some of the gross defects in American medicine. There are critical shortages of physicians in the rural and the central urban areas. New doctors are not being trained in sufficient numbers because of the costs of medical training and insufficient space in medical schools to accommodate the demand. The infant-mortality rate in the United States is 22 per 1,000 births. Thirteen countries—including Japan, Australia, Canada, and many western European nations—have lower rates. For a people with our resources, we should be able to produce medical care second to none in the world. An environmentally concerned citizen does not neglect the most important species in his environment—his fellow man.

Welfare

There were 25.4 million people in the United States in 1968 who were classified as poor. Of that number about 4.6 million were more than sixty-five years old—about 25 percent of all elderly people. Children under eighteen constitute another large group of poor people: About 10.7 million children are classified as poor ("Profile of the Poor," 1970). Another category of the poor includes families with dependent children in households headed by women. These three categories of poor people suggest who most needs assistance from our government and other social agencies. If this and upcoming generations care about their environment, then they cannot ignore the elderly, children, and mothers of dependent children who constitute part of this environment.

The editors of *Saturday Review* have described the welfare problem in the United States in lucid terms:

> One hallmark of a civilized society is its willingness to care for its poor, ill, elderly, dependent young, and permanently handicapped. Since adoption of the Elizabethan Poor Laws in England more than three centuries ago, Western societies have recognized such care as a public responsibility. Yet, it has become increasingly apparent in recent years that the chief governmental vehicle in the United States for providing such care—Public Welfare—has broken down, both in ability to achieve humanitarian ends and in public capacity to finance it. ("Welfare," 1970)

At a time in our national history when we are striving to extricate our armed forces from Vietnam and when new directions are being sought for the human talent and material resources of this nation, a reformed program of care for the needy is imperative.

Various plans have been proposed. President Nixon's Family Assistance Plan is designed to permit individuals to contribute to the full extent of their capabilities. A look at the three categories that constitute a majority of poor people makes it clear that work is virtually impossible for many of them. A mother of small children who heads a household may not be able to work. Many people over sixty-five are unable to work because of their age and health. Children under eighteen should be in school. Requiring that welfare recipients be employed is unrealistic.

Consciousness of poverty is something that the elementary school can help to develop in children. People throughout the country must become concerned enough to give this national, state, and local responsibility precedence over other needs.

Military Expenditures

This nation can never solve its domestic problems—like inadequate housing, inner-city blight, inadequate health services, public welfare, and inadequate transportation—while so much of the national budget is spent on defense. Blackaby (1970) has called the arms race the world's "greatest waste of resources" and its "most pressing danger." In the past twenty years military spending has absorbed close to 8 percent of the world's total output. Although this figure is distressing, it is even more discouraging to realize that American military expenditures were $79.5 billion in 1968. Although there was a decline in the percentage of the total budget allocated to national defense in 1971, the figure still represented 37 percent of the total. No other country approaches this rate of military expenditure. In 1968 the U.S.S.R. spent $18.6 billion (at official basic exchange rates; Blackaby, 1970). The United States spent 8.5 percent of its 1968 Gross National Product on defense. No other large nation approached this percentage, though figures for the Soviet Union were not available (Alexander, 1969).

Demands for military expenditures have been strangling the American economy. President Dwight D. Eisenhower warned in 1960 that the military-industrial complex makes itself felt in every city, every statehouse, and every office of the Federal government. The influence of the military and of all kinds of industries that rely on defense contracts permeates the entire nation. McCarthy (1968) has called attention to the increasing militarization of our foreign policy and the tendency to assess political problems in military terms.

Many prominent scientists and other citizens protested strongly when the army began to prepare an antiballistic-missile site near Chicago. Citizens have a right to be concerned when nuclear warheads are installed in their back yards.

Concerned citizens of the United States must make known their feelings about continued massive expenditure of national resources for devices like antiballistic missiles that are of questionable defensive value. As long as the United States continues to pile up military reserves, the likelihood of war increases. Application of our resources and human abilities to constructive assistance to developing nations might have more beneficial long-range effects.

School children should know and be concerned about the amounts of money that the United States spends for defense compared with those spent by other nations. They also should know how the national budget is distributed. Understanding our responsibilities as world citizens should arouse concern about national values that must be reordered.

INVESTIGATIONS

1. Describe the kind of city that you would like to live in. What kind of services would you want from that city, and how could they be supplied?

2. Try to envision what your community will be like in 1985 if its present rates of growth, pollution, resource consumption, abuse of people, and general lack of environmental concern continue. How would a person have to live in order to survive in such a community?

3. Now list all the changes that must be made now in order to avert such a disaster. What alterations must be made in the ways that people travel, their consumption of products and services, and their disposition of finished products?

4. Try to identify agencies, government bodies, private firms, and individuals in your community who can exert influence to achieve the changes listed.

5. Make contact with appropriate officials to find out what action is being taken to bring about these changes. How is your city adjusting to the changing needs for transportation? What provisions are being made for recovery and reuse of wastes?

6. It has been suggested that automobiles be banned from downtown in the not too distant future. Identify problems that this ban will create for people in your community. What steps will have to be taken to provide transportation then?

7. How are wrecked and junked automobiles disposed of in your community? Can you take a picture of an auto graveyard? Imagine ways in which cars could be disposed of and reused.

8. What kind of school environment would you like to have? Are there places in your community where you could learn better than in your classroom? What are the obstacles to using an outdoor classroom?

9. Looking ahead to 1975 and 1980, tell where you think government money should be spent on transportation. Airplanes? Trains? Cars? Supersonic transport? Subways?

10. Find out about different possible substitutes for the internal-combustion engine. What are the difficulties in developing a steam-driven car? An electric car? A car with any other kind of external-combustion engine?

11. Look at the film *Pandora's Easy Open Pop-Top Box* (available free from Environmental Control Administration, 12720 Twinbrook Parkway, Rockville, Maryland 20852), which shows the dramatic effects of uncontrolled urbanization. What urban controls are suggested by this film?

12. Now look at the film *Green City* (available from Stuart Finley Productions, 3428 Mansfield Road, Falls Church, Virginia 22041), and see what civic action can be taken to preserve green and open spaces in a growing city.

13. Try to imagine what it is like to have to live on the $1,600 a year proposed as the minimum annual income. Without revealing specific family incomes, mothers can tell children how much is spent in their families each month for food, for clothing, for electricity, for fuel. Which of these items could you do without if your family income were stopped?

REFERENCES

Alexander, Archibald S. "The Cost of World Armaments," *Scientific American,* 221:21–27, October 1969.

Blackaby, Frank. "History's Greatest Dead End," *Saturday Review,* 53:19–21, March 14, 1970.

Cloud, Preston. "Government and the Climate for Science," *Science Teacher,* 36:19–22, December 1969.

Cousins, Norman. "How to Get Nowhere: Need for Modern Mass Transit Systems," *Saturday Review,* 53:49, April 4, 1970.

Gavin, J. M. & A. Hadley. "The Crises of the Cities: The Battle We Can Win," *Saturday Review,* 51:30–34, February 24, 1968.

Glass, Bentley. "For Full Technological Assessment," *Science,* 165:755, August 1969.

Grinstead, Robert R. "The New Resource," *Environment,* 12:2–17, December 1970.

"How to Dispose of Cans and Bottles," *Good Housekeeping,* 171:154–155, September 1970.

Hudson, James W. "We Can Build Space Age Cities Now," *National Wildlife,* 8:4–9, August 1970.

Javits, Jacob. "Can President Nixon Stop the Arms Race?" *Saturday Review*, 52:14–17, March 1, 1969.

Lowry, W. P. "The Climate of Cities," *Scientific American*, 219:15–23, August 1967.

McCarthy, Eugene J. "The Power of the Pentagon," *Saturday Review*, 51:8–10, December 21, 1968.

McQuade, Walter. "Downtown Is Looking Up," *Fortune*, 81:132–142, February 1970.

Moynihan, Daniel P. "One Step We Must Take," *Saturday Review*, 53:20–23, May 23, 1970.

Mumford, Lewis. *The Urban Prospect.* New York: Harcourt, 1968.

Nuessle, Virginia D. & Robert W. Holcomb. "Will the SST Pollute the Stratosphere?" *Science*, 168:1562, June 26, 1970.

Pettigrew, Thomas F. "The Metropolitan Educational Park," *Science Teacher*, 36:23–26, December 1969.

"Profile of the Poor," *Saturday Review*, 53:23, May 23, 1970.

Rathjens, George W. "The Dynamics of the Arms Race," *Scientific American*, 220:15–25, April 1969.

Ribicoff, Abraham. "The Healthiest Nation Myth," *Saturday Review*, 53:18–20, August 22, 1970.

Spilhaus, Athelstan. "The Experimental City," *Daedalus*, 96:1129–1141, Fall 1967.

Spilhaus, Athelstan. "Why Have Cities?" *Science Teacher*, 36:16–18, December 1969.

Spofford, Walter O., Jr. "Closing the Gap in Waste Management," *Environmental Science and Technology*, 4:1108–1114, December 1970.

"SST: Commercial Race or Technology Experiment?" *Science*, 169:352, July 24, 1970.

Stueck, Hans J. "Urban Transit Model," *Saturday Review*, 53:62–63, December 5, 1970.

Tobin, R. L. "Communicating by Rail: Metroliner Shuttling Daily between New York and Washington," *Saturday Review*, 52:51–52, February 8, 1969.

U.S. Bureau of the Budget. *The Budget in Brief: Fiscal Year 1971.* Washington, D.C.: Government Printing Office, 1971.

Volpe, J. A. "Urban Transportation Tomorrow," *American City*, 84:59–62, November 1969.

Von Eckardt, Wolf. "Creative Urbanists," *Saturday Review*, 53:48–49, August 1, 1970.

Von Eckardt, Wolf. "People, Yes; Cars, No," *Saturday Review*, 53:62–63, October 3, 1970.

"Welfare: Time for Reform," *Saturday Review*, 53:19, May 23, 1970.

York, Herbert. "Military Technology and National Security," *Scientific American*, 221:17–30, August 1969.

part three / *challenge for survival*

chapter 9 / practical ideas and techniques for teachers

In planning and organizing activities in environmental education, the teacher should use a variety of human and material resources—and especially imagination.

RESPONSIBILITIES IN AN "INQUIRY-CENTERED" PROGRAM

One of the most remarkable features of human beings is that their behavior tends to mirror their environments. Children thus behave as they sense that their environment demands. If we want children to develop rational powers and to learn the structure of ecology and related disciplines by investigation, then their classroom and school environments must encourage investigation. The Educational Policies Commission has described such a classroom: "The school which develops the ability to think is itself a place where thought is respected and where humane values implicit in rationality are honored. It has an atmosphere conducive to thinking and it rewards its pupils for progress toward the goals it values" (Educational Policies Commission, 1961).

In the "inquiry-centered" classroom the child participates actively in the learning process. Introducing a pupil to his environment by means of encouraging inquiry enables him to begin building a conception of the environment that will continue throughout his life. Renner and Ragan (1968) have identified three principles to guide teachers in establishing environments conducive to investigation:

First, teachers should listen to the children. We teachers must constantly remind ourselves that our principal goal is to assist children to learn why they know what they know (to learn how to learn); we must remember that this goal can best be achieved if children's own discoveries about topics under consideration are recognized and incorporated.

Second, teachers must themselves be investigators. An investigation is any activity designed to secure information that will enable the investigator to describe a phenomenon or understand it better. Most children can easily identify phonies. A teacher cannot successfully ask children to make hypotheses if he himself never guesses or allows critical analysis of his guesses. He should be continually involved in questioning, probing, and assisting pupils in data collection and analysis.

Third, appropriate resources necessary for investigation must be provided. If a pupil is to determine whether or not different types of plants need different amounts of water, several different types of plants are required. If chalkboard, chalk, and "good, long looks" are substituted for actual experience with nature, then children must learn through constructing abstractions. Yet the research of Piaget and others has revealed that elementary-school pupils have difficulty with gross abstractions and generalizations. Emphasis should therefore be placed upon verifying or disproving hypotheses based on concrete data.

Improving Questioning Skills

Suchman's (1966) research involves children questioning the teacher instead of the teacher questioning children. A set of twenty-five color films were made in eight-millimeter cartridges, silent with no captions. Each film contains a puzzling event that students attempt to explain. Some sample titles are *Ball and Ring Demonstration, The Shrinking Balloon, Boiling by Cooling, The Balloon in the Jar,* and *The Ice Cubes.* Each film viewing is followed by an inquiry session in which students ask data-gathering questions that are answered by the teacher. Inquiry sessions follow these simple rules:

1. The questions should be phrased in order that they can be answered yes or no.
2. Once called upon, a student may ask as many questions as he or she wishes before yielding the floor.
3. The teacher does not answer yes or no to statements of theories or to questions that attempt to obtain the teacher's approval of a theory.
4. Any student can test any theory at any time.
5. Any time the students feel a need to confer with one another without the teacher's presence, they may call a conference.

6. Inquirers should be able to work with experimental kits, idea books, or resource books at any time they feel the need.

(The reader should see also Piaget & Inhelder, 1958, and Washton, 1967.)

The ways in which a teacher uses questions has a significant influence on children's development of inquiry skills. Here are some tips for teachers:

1. Plan some specific questions before the lesson.
2. Ask question before designating which child should answer.
3. Ask an individual child to respond to each question.
4. Vary the questions, both in difficulty and type.
5. Use words that stimulate creative thinking: "compare," "observe," "criticize," "interpret," and the like.
6. Emphasize specifics, rather than generalities.
7. Avoid asking "yes or no" questions.
8. Avoid putting too many questions into one statement.
9. Ask some questions that require children to use scientific processes like hypothesizing, predicting, operational definition, evaluation, and so on.

LEARNING LABORATORIES

As emphasized throughout this book, the school should be an environmental model that enables children to engage in various multisensory experiences. Provision should be made for both indoor and outdoor experiences.

Classroom "interest centers" facilitate the inquiry process and allow children to make their own observations. Interest centers may include collections made by the children and teachers. Aquariums, terrariums, small caged animals, and potted plants are good examples. In addition to their instructional value, the centers provide children with opportunities to accept responsibility, to develop pride of ownership, and to express curiosity.

Classroom collections may consist of leaves, rocks, wood samples, bird feathers, or any of an endless array of natural objects. The composition of the collection is less important than the involvement of the children in the collecting process. Class collections may result from field trips or individual efforts. After the "collectables" are brought into the classrooms, the children can be organized into small groups to identify, label, and mount them. The identification process offers an excellent opportunity for the teacher to introduce principles of research. Available materials like books, encyclopedias, and pictures may help to identify specimens. The teacher should provide proper materials for labeling and mounting. It is helpful to remember that children prefer bright colors for backing material.

The aquarium is a valuable teaching tool and an endless source of pleasure for children. Lowery (1969) has suggested that it be used for observation and study of aquatic plants, animals, and their relations. A properly equipped aquarium requires little maintenance and is simple to prepare. It should be square or rectangular because round or oval bowls provide less oxygen for the fish. It should be placed on a sturdy base. Any sand or gravel placed in it should be washed thoroughly first. The children may pour water through sand or gravel until it comes through clear. The water for the aquarium should be allowed to stand for several days so that the chlorine can evaporate. Water should be poured into the aquarium very slowly to avoid clouding. When the aquarium is partly filled, the plants should be added. Then the rest of the water is added, and selected fish are placed in the aquarium. The water must be at the proper temperature for the type of fish selected. Fresh-water fish require temperatures of 65–70 degrees Fahrenheit, whereas tropical fish require temperatures of 73–78 degrees Fahrenheit.

All the children should participate in selecting fish for the aquarium. They may select on the basis of size, compatibility, hardiness, beauty, or ability to keep the tank clean. The teacher must provide access to data that will help children learn what they need to know to make wise decisions.

A terrarium can be easily constructed in a gallon glass jar with a wide mouth. An effective terrarium must be practically self-perpetuating. Careful attention should be given to the compatibility of the animals and plants to be placed inside. The teacher should discuss with the children what should be included. Simple preparation of a terrarium includes six steps. First, a small amount of plaster of paris is mixed to form a base; it is placed inside the jar on one side. Second, a layer of gravel is added to provide for drainage. Third, approximately three inches of soil and a small container of water are added. Fourth, plant moss, ferns, wildflowers, or other small plants are planted in the soil. Fifth, a small animal like a snake, turtle, salamander, or frog is included. Sixth, close the top of the jar, and add water only when necessary. If the terrarium is properly arranged it will maintain its own hydrologic cycle.

Some small animals thrive in the classroom, providing endless enjoyment for children. Gerbils, guinea pigs, snakes, hermit crabs, frogs, turtles, and mice are all appropriate. Caged animals require water, a little food, and a soft floor covering in the cages.

The classroom should be equipped with many materials, including books, magazines, films, filmstrips, programmed texts, and microprojections. Attractive materials, supported by thought-provoking questions, can create interest. Here are a few suggestions for displays:

1. Select the ecological concepts and principles that children are to learn.

2. Engage children in collecting pictures and materials for display.
3. Ask thought-provoking questions.
4. Use attractive, eye-catching lettering and materials.
5. Use the display as a teaching tool.

(See Appendix A for various resource suggestions.)

Radio and television are continually contributing to children's scientific information, but research indicates that television viewing alone is not as effective as when accompanied by competent classroom guidance. In addition to closed-circuit television some network commercial programs and series are very helpful. For example, *Animal Secrets* (NBC), *Wild Kingdom* (NBC), *Discovery* (ABC), and *21st Century* (CBS) are all excellent.

Effective learning often requires trips outside the classroom to observe natural phenomena. Outdoor experiences should be well planned and flexible enough to facilitate discovery.

When time and transportation are limited, children may simply use the school grounds for observation and experiment. They may observe the erosion of a badly washed bank and propose measures to prevent future erosion. Students can profit from a search for animal life on the grounds. They may find birds, insects, rodents, and so on. Other projects could include beautification of the grounds to promote pride in the appearance of the school.

School nature sites and parks provide opportunities for more extensive investigation and experimentation. The development of a nature site requires a great deal of cooperative effort. The area must be mapped and any possible hazards marked. Kellers (1970) has noted that the use of parks is preferable because no extra personnel and funds are needed. School systems without access to park facilities available must develop their own sites.

Parks and nature sites can be put to many uses, including:

1. Observation of animal homes.
2. Observation of the effects of water and wind upon the terrain.
3. Study of animal life.
4. Observation of the life cycle of forests, fields, bogs, and so on.

It is most important that students study relations in the real world. Field trips can be very valuable in this respect if these preliminary measures are taken:

1. Carefully define the major objectives of the trip.
2. Make a preliminary visit to the site to ensure that these objectives will be met.

3. Well before the trip arrange for parental permission, transportation, scheduling, safety provisions, materials, money, and so on. Ask parental assistance if necessary.
4. Avoid trying to accomplish too much in a limited time period.
5. Emphasize collection of data and related "inquiry" skills.
6. Provide for feedback and evaluation of the excursion.
7. Consult the science division of the state department of education for a list of appropriate parks, lakes, and selected field settings for exploration.
8. Relate field experiences to continuing classroom instruction.

Human Resources and Agencies

Children are most likely to behave as do the people with whom they associate. Parents, other adults, and siblings constitute a reference group, to which the child turns for approval and support. According to Brookover and Ericksen (1969), a member of this group is a *significant other*, an individual who influences a person's beliefs about himself. We immediately think of the teacher as a significant other. In the formal education of a child, parents may be equally if not more important.

Parents are key resources in education. They should be partners with teachers, and learning situations should be structured to bring parents into the school setting. Parents can

1. Serve as teachers' aides.
2. Assist on field trips.
3. Discuss pertinent topics of environmental concern.
4. Construct classroom models, materials, interest centers, and so on.
5. Serve as media assistants.
6. Influence the P.T.A. to support environmental education.
7. Assist in development of school nature sites.
8. Provide positive reinforcement at home of the school's efforts.

Significant others may include a minister, a Boy or Girl Scout Leader, or any adult who identifies with and assists a child in his personal development. An environmental education program should involve forest rangers, conservation specialists, sanitation personnel, managers of water-purification plants, members of air-pollution control boards, U.S. Department of Agriculture personnel, ecologists, biologists, health-department personnel, engineers, lawyers, meteorologists, and many others who can make significant contributions to environmental-education programs in elementary schools. It is useful to maintain a file of such people, noting when they are available and their special fields of competence.

There are many state and Federal agencies that participate actively in environmental programs. Some offer specialized training for teachers, materials, and expert assistance. (See Appendix A for a listing of some of these agencies.)

SUGGESTIONS FOR IN-SERVICE TRAINING OF TEACHERS

The fully functioning professional educator regards training as a continuous process of self-improvement throughout his working life. In order to help elementary-school teachers design and implement environmental education for children, continuous in-service training should be provided. Teachers should be informed about current environmental issues, as well as keeping up to date with scientific and social advances. Thorough knowledge of the school setting and the surrounding "environments" is most important. Except for some formal courses in ecology and related sciences, in-service programs can best be conducted locally.

They should focus upon helping teachers to *use* knowledge of children, knowledge of related disciplines, environmental problems and issues, human and material resources, local "environments" like schools and so on, curricular design, and instructional strategies. College, university, and state education consultants can help teachers in local communities work on "real" problems. Teachers should be released for periods of time during the school day to participate in in-service training; late-afternoon sessions should be avoided when possible. Teachers should also be encouraged to participate in summer workshops, institutes, and similar activities. Principles of teacher assignment and use should be used effectively. A library of environmental-education materials should be provided for staff use. All in-service training should be carefully planned and evaluated.

In-service training should also be provided for administrators and special school personnel, with attention to arousing "citizen awareness" and support of environmental education.

VALUE ANALYSIS AND SENSITIVITY TO THE ENVIRONMENT

Most environmental problems are primarily problems of human behavior. Insensitivity to the environment can be documented by research. "Awareness" may be defined as the ability to describe processes occurring in one's life space. Positive action is guided by a person's awareness and his system of values. How sensitive are we to the problems of solid waste, air pollution, automobiles as major polluters, the "spaceship philosophy" of dumping waste materials, and population control?

American education is currently far more strongly oriented toward cognitive learning than toward affective learning (Estvan, p. 300). Instruction and evaluation are most often geared toward measuring what a pupil knows and how well he can perform, rather than what he feels and values and how well he performs in everyday life.

An attempt to develop one set of values for all individuals is not the answer. It is the school's responsibility to help children understand the sources of their values, to analyze values, and to recognize alternatives.

There are too many children in school who do not learn as well as they could because they are uncertain about values. In different socio-economic settings values will vary tremendously between home and school and among various populations.

How does the teacher deal with these differences? Teachers should not force their own value structures on students, give moral lessons, or assign students to memorize lists of values.

> In general, this means that we must find ways of creating school and classroom atmosphere which facilitates the process of exploration and discovery of personal meaning—where there can be a freeing, expanding and changing of perception. Students need to have many choices; when they discover something of interest, they need to have plenty of time to work at it. Self-selection in an environment rich in materials, where students sense that how they feel and what they think are important, can be extremely effective in helping students to become more fully functioning. Through acceptance and trust, particularly, teachers play a strategic role in this learning process. (Association for Supervision and Curriculum Development, 1962)

The decision to help students develop systems of value analysis in itself represents a major value judgment, however. Educators are so caught up in a web of value judgments that they cannot help but pass some of these judgments on to their students. Teachers influence development of values by their own everyday behavior. Many teachers are almost totally unaware of how much their activities and words influence students. As this incidental, or accidental, influence occurs in all educational settings, there is no question that value education already exists.

The important question is "How can educators design a rational system by which students can analyze various value orientations?" Values are part of the education of the total person. According to Nystrand and Cunningham (1969) the curriculum must reflect a humanistic approach to values that includes continuing appraisal of the environment, one's own aspirations, and the aspirations of others. This notion of interaction with others is central to the analysis of values.

As Fenton (1966) has suggested, certain behavioral values (as expressed, for example, in specific rules for classroom behavior) and certain procedural values (as expressed, for example, in the choice of logical analysis over illogic) are necessary to effective teaching. There are many general goals (like promoting the dignity of the individual, effective development of moral values, and intelligent use of natural resources) on which most Americans agree. But these goals do not easily lend themselves to instructional strategies. We must translate broad social goals into specific behavior expected of students. Fraenkel (1969) has identified certain types of behavior that may serve as evidence that students recognize the dignity of the individual:

1. He does not interrupt others in conversation.
2. He avoids monopolizing conversation with his own arguments.
3. He revises his own opinions when others' arguments are convincing.
4. He does not humiliate or embarrass others, regardless of their social or economic status.

We must develop more precise strategies for developing this kind of behavior.

One sorely neglected dimension of value education is exploration of core values in American culture, as well as in various ethnic, regional, and local subcultures. In our complex society teachers must often serve as mediators between children and the larger culture. They must help children to evaluate behavior sanctioned by society. Students should learn that subcultural differences are a positive element in American society.

More research is necessary to determine the best ways to achieve these goals. Higgins (1970) explored value development among fourth-graders, using an open-ended instrument and objective classification of responses. She concluded that this method is a valuable means of making teachers aware of pupils' needs for clarification of value position. Awareness of pupils' needs is the necessary first step to the development of specific instructional programs.

It is even more difficult to specify objectives and instructional strategies for affective training than for cognitive training. But such difficulty certainly should not cause abandonment of such training. On the contrary, children's tremendous need for assistance in developing attitudes and values should challenge professionals to seek new strategies. For specific assistance with this task, the reader should consult Krathwohl and his colleagues (1964).

Bauer (1970) has identified several skills appropriate to value analysis: recognizing the values held by oneself and others, as well as their sources; identifying and analyzing value conflicts; assessing possible alternatives, and learning to take stands.

Shaftel (1967) has strongly recommended role playing to help children solve interpersonal and intergroup difficulties intelligently, sensitively, and responsibly. Through enactment of roles in carefully selected problem stories, students may develop understanding and respect for the value orientations of various cultures other than their own.

Bibliotheraphy has been effective in helping children to learn affectively. It emphasizes the usefulness of reading in helping children to understand and accept themselves and to gain insight into various behavior patterns. This technique is described by Crosby (1963) and Junell (1969).

Analysis of "critical incidents in teaching" or stories of conflict situations can be most helpful, provided that students understand system and objectivity. They should be helped to ask and answer why, what, and what are the alternatives? They read a story in which an individual becomes involved in a crisis or conflict. They must place themselves in his position and decide what course of action he should follow. Such activities should be directed toward developing generalizations that can serve as guides to affective behavior.

Raths and his colleagues' (1966) "value-clarifying method" is also useful. The basic principle is to respond to students so as to stimulate them to clarify their own thinking and behavior and thus their values. Every teacher can refine his question-and-response techniques to promote such clarification and thus influence significant behavioral change. Typically, the teacher responds to a student's remark with a question designed to force him to analyze his own value system. Raths and his colleagues have listed thirty responses that serve this purpose. Here are a few:

1. How did you feel when that happened?
2. Have you felt this way for a long time?
3. Where would that idea lead? What would be its consequences?
4. Would you really do that, or are you just talking?
5. Did you have to choose that? Was it a free choice?
6. Is there a purpose behind this activity?

For the teacher who is really concerned about improving his value instruction, Raths and his colleagues have described several techniques: discussions to clarify values, role playing, zigzag lessons, playing the devil's advocate, and open-ended questions.

The development of a system of value analysis is as important to the student as is any academic subject. A teacher must have flexible attitudes and a desire to help his students develop as complete human beings.

In his planning and teaching he must strive for a balance between the cognitive and affective domains of learning. Such balance is prerequisite to development of strategies for facilitating value growth in positive directions.

SUMMARY

The teacher has a major responsibility to provide an inquiry-centered environment that encourages investigations. The teacher should be an investigator, providing a model for the students. He should be continuously involved in questioning, probing, and assisting pupils in data collection and analysis.

The school and grounds should serve as an environmental model that enables children to engage in multisensory experiences. The teacher should utilize the services of a variety of resource personnel in addition to engaging in continuous in-service training experiences. Since most of our environmental problems are a result of man's insensitivity to the environment, greater emphasis should be given to the development of positive values relative to the environment. The teacher should help students employ a variety of value analysis skills. By engaging the learner in processes of value analysis the teacher facilitates positive value orientations toward the environment.

REFERENCES

Association for Supervision and Curriculum Development. *Perceiving, Behaving, Becoming: A New Focus for Education.* Washington, D.C.: National Education Association, 1962.

Bauer, Nancy W. "Can you Teach Values?" *Instructor*, August–September 1970.

Brookover, Wilbur B. & Edsel L. Ericksen. *Society, Schools and Learning.* Boston: Allyn & Bacon, 1969.

Crosby, Muriel (ed.). *Reading Ladders for Human Relations*, 4th ed. Washington, D.C.: American Council on Education, 1963.

Educational Policies Commission. *The Central Purpose of American Education.* Washington, D.C.: National Education Association, 1961.

Estvan, Frank. *Social Studies in a Changing World.* New York: Harcourt, 1968.

Fenton, Edwin. *Teaching the New Social Studies in Secondary Schools: An Inductive Approach.* New York: Holt, 1966.

Fraenkel, Jack R. "Value Education in the Social Studies," *Phi Delta Kappan*, 50:457–461, April 1969.

Higgins, Elizabeth B. "An Exploratory Investigation of the Valuing Processes of a Group of Fourth-Grade Pupils," *Educational Leadership*, 27:706–712, April 1970.

Junell, Joseph S. "Do Teachers Have the Right to Indoctrinate?" *Phi Delta Kappan*, 51:182–185, December 1969.

Kellers, K. T. "Organizing Outdoor Classrooms in the Park System," *The Science Teacher*, 37:56–59, January 1970.

Krathwohl, David R., Benjamin S. Bloom & Bertram B. Masia. *Taxonomy of Educational Objectives. Handbook II. Affective Domain*. New York: McKay, 1964.

Lowery, Lawrence F. "The Vivarium," *Science and Children*, 7:22–25, October 1969.

Nystrand, Raphael O. & Luvern L. Cunningham. "Organizing Schools to Develop Humane Capabilities," in Mary-Margaret Scoby & Grace Graham (eds.), *To Nurture Humaneness*. Washington, D.C.: National Education Association, 1969.

Piaget, Jean & Bärbel Inhelder. *The Growth of Logical Thinking*. New York: Basic Books, 1958.

Raths, Louis E., Merrill Harmin & Sidney B. Simon. *Values and Teaching*. Columbus, O.: Merrill, 1966.

Renner, John W. & William B. Ragan. *Teaching Science in the Elementary School*. New York: Harper, 1968.

Shaftel, Fannie R. *Role Playing for Social Values: Decision Making in the Social Studies*. Englewood Cliffs, N.J.: Prentice-Hall, 1967.

Suchman, J. Richard. *Putting Inquiry into Science: Learning-Inquiry Development Program*. Chicago: Science Research Associates, 1966.

Washton, Nathan S. "Teaching Science Creatively: A Taxonomy of Pupil Questions," *Science Education*, 51:428–431, No. 5, December 1967.

chapter 10 / environmental education: a challenge to survival

Careful study of the first nine chapters should help the reader to understand crucial environmental problems and issues, basic concepts and processes of ecology, curriculum design, and considerations in planning and conducting environmental experiences for children. An educator who is informed and concerned has taken a major step toward positive action.

EDUCATION FOR SURVIVAL

As educators we face a tremendous challenge and a tremendous responsibility to take positive action. Environmental education today is no less than education for survival. We must be saved from ourselves. As Pogo said, "We have met the enemy and he is us." Our environmental crisis arises largely from a "caveman mentality" that assumes that the environment can absorb everything that man dumps in it. Training citizens to design and maintain an environment that does not now exist involves some rather significant changes in basic cultural values. For example, Grinstead (1970) has suggested that two changes in official attitudes are critical if we are serious about reusing waste materials. First, waste-material industries must receive encouragement at least equal to that given raw-material industries. Second, feedback between the disposal and manufacturing processes must be established. Recycling may eventually become as highly valued as is basic production.

Wagar (1970) has declared that values like growth, laissez-faire, economic efficiency, and specialization—values woven into the very fabric of our economic order—are also at the heart of our problems. He has suggested two basic choices: We can voluntarily limit our growth and other impacts upon the environment; the limiting factor would be *attraction* to a life style based on space, abundance, freedom of many kinds, and a broad variety of alternative opportunities. Or we can permit pollution and congestion to continue until they are stopped by *hardships*, limiting factors not of our choosing.

Fischer (September 1969) has proposed treating the concept of survival as an organizing principle in many fields of scholarly inquiry and curriculum planning from kindergarten through the university. He has also proposed (November 1969) that a master plan for "building a second America" be based on achieving environmental quality. Planners would draw heavily on human ecology, which teaches us the consequences of our actions. Boyer (1971) has strongly urged educators to plan relevant education for survival, defined as vitally connected either to the conditions that sustain life or to those that give life meaning. He believes that education in health, food production, nutrition, population control, and war prevention is the kind of education that can help to sustain life.

POSITIVE DEVELOPMENTS: A CALL FOR ACTION

Warnings that we are in grave danger of irreversible catastrophe have come from many social scientists, biologists, and physicists, including distinguished thinkers like René Dubos, Buckminster Fuller, Loren Eisely, George Wald, Paul Ehrlich, and Barry Commoner. Recent developments indicate that we are beginning to respond positively to these warnings. First, significant Federal legislation has been passed. The Environmental Education Act established an Office of Environmental Education within the Office of Education. The program calls for improved curricula and materials and authorizes the Commissioner of Education to make grants to nonprofit corporations engaged in developing them. Additional Federal, state, and local legislation is under consideration. Second, enforcement of existing environmental laws has been improved; at least, litigation against companies and individuals who are polluting the environment has increased. Third, attention to environmental problems in the mass media is increasing awareness among our citizens. Fourth, attention to environmental problems and issues among political, governmental, business, and industrial leaders is encouraging. Fifth, ever-increasing concern is being expressed by individual citizens. Finally, recent efforts to develop new processes of recycling have had good results.

American educators are also seeking environmental improvement. At "Education and the Environment in the Americas," an international meeting in Washington, D.C., cosponsored by the American Association of Colleges for Teacher Education (A.A.C.T.E.) and the Organization of

American States (O.A.S.), more than 200 educators from nearly every nation in the Western Hemisphere sought effective educational responses to problems of pollution and depletion of resources.

Second, environmental-education curricula are currently being developed at Federal, state, and local levels. An encouraging example is a recent proposal by which ("New Jersey Has Pollution Problems," 1971) a Federal grant would establish New Jersey as a demonstration laboratory in environmental education for the entire nation. The master plan calls for establishment of an advisory board representing the various "publics" of the state. The board would direct a model center for environmental education charged with developing curricula for elementary and secondary schools, colleges and universities, and adults. The center would also serve as a clearinghouse for information on environmental education and related activities. It has also been proposed that every college student be required to take a course in environmental studies and that similar courses be provided for adults. An excellent example of a teachers' guide to environmental education has recently been developed in North Carolina (see Appendix A).

The time for positive action on the environment was yesterday. The hour is late. As responsible educators, we should not prophesy doom but lead positive action. To meet this challenge we must plan and teach environmental concepts and processes at every point in the educational progression but especially during the formative years—in the elementary schools.

REFERENCES

Boyer, William H. "Education for Survival," *Phi Delta Kappan*, 52:258–262, January 1971.

Fischer, John. "Survival U: Prospectus for a Really Relevant University," *Harper's*, 239:12–22, September 1969.

Fischer, John. "Planning for the Second America," *Harper's*, 239:21–26, November 1969.

Grinstead, Robert R. "The New Resource," *Environment*, 10:3–17, December 1970.

"New Jersey Has Pollution Problems," *Phi Delta Kappan*, 52:322–323, January 1971.

Wagar, J. Alan. "The Challenge of Environmental Education," *Today's Education*, 59:15–18, December 1970.

glossary

Adaptation. The process by which an organism or a species changes in order to live in its environment. This process may take many millions of years of evolution and natural selection.

Aerobic Organism. An animal or plant that requires atmospheric oxygen for respiration.

Anaerobic Organism. An animal or plant that can live in an environment in which little or no atmospheric oxygen is available.

Aquifer. A subterranean layer of porous soil through which ground water travels slowly during the hydrologic cycle.

Biodegradable. The characteristic of any substance that breaks down rapidly through the action of organisms. Vegetable peelings, uprooted weeds, and grass clippings are biodegradable; aluminum cans, some plastics, and DDT are not.

Bioenergetics. The biochemistry of energy transformations.

Biomass. The amount of living material in a defined ecosystem measured by weight.

Biome. A climatically controlled area including a number of different communities. The biomes constitute the major ecological regions of the world such as the tundra, the desert, the grasslands, and the various forests.

Biosphere. That part of the earth in which life exists. This terrestrial envelope extends more than 10,000 meters deep in the ocean, and as high as 10,000 meters in the atmosphere; it includes the earth's land, water, and atmosphere, where all organisms live.

Biotic Community. A part of the biosphere set aside for study but that also interacts with its surroundings.

Carbon Cycle. Carbon is an element that is present in all organic substances.

Carbon dioxide in the atmosphere is used by plants in the process of photosynthesis. It is converted into carbonates in animals. Both producers and consumers discard carbon-bearing wastes. Saprovores cause organisms and their wastes to decay, releasing carbon again in the form of carbon dioxide.

Carcinogen. A substance that can produce cancer.

Chlorinated Hydrocarbons. A class of synthetic organic insecticides that do not break down in the environment but are recycled through food chains. They are soluble in fats and tend to accumulate in animals at the top of the food chain: birds, larger animals, and man. Aldrin, dieldrin, endrin, chlordane, heptachlor, toxaphene, lindane, DDT, DDD, and TDE are members of this group.

Compost. Organic wastes produced by decomposing garbage and vegetation mixed with soil. Bacteria in the soil help to decompose the waste.

Consumer. A user of food from the producer in the energy pyramid. Plants are producers, whereas animals can be primary, secondary, or tertiary consumers. Each higher consumption level obtains a degree less energy than was captured in the preceding one.

Decibel. A unit of measure of sound-pressure level. The lower threshold of clear hearing is between 50 and 75 decibels; the threshold of discomfort is at about 120 decibels, and the threshold of pain is at 130 decibels.

Decomposer. A bacterium, fungus, or other organism that breaks down dead plants and animals and their wastes.

Ecology. In scientific use, a study of living things in relation to their environment and to one another.

Ecosystem. An integrated natural system, including both the biotic community and the abiotic environment of rocks, water, air, and other nonliving things.

Effluent. The discharge from sewage-treatment plants, smokestacks, and nuclear-power plants. Often this effluence is polluted.

Emphysema. A disease of the lungs in which the alveoli, or air sacs, are permanently changed so that less surface area is available for oxygen transfer. The individual's ability to breath is severely impaired.

Energy Cycle. The process by which plants convert solar energy into organic compounds that are consumed by animals, which are then returned to the atmosphere through decay and deposition. The amount of energy stored in the earth has been increased through the earth's 4.5 billion-year history, but man is now rapidly depleting that energy store.

Environment. An organism's entire surroundings, both organic and inorganic.

Estuary. A coastal body of water where salt and fresh water intermingles. River mouths, bays, lagoons, marshes, sounds, and tidal flats are all estuaries. The water is said to be "brackish."

Eutrophic Lake. Shallow, old lake, with high productivity of algae.

Eutrophication. The gradual build-up or increase of organic compounds in an aquatic ecosystem over a long period of time. Phosphates in waste water may provide excessive nutrients, resulting in rapid growth of algae.

Food Chain. An energy pathway from producers through first-order consumers (herbivores), second-order consumers (carnivores), to third-order consumers, as from grass to rabbit to fox to buzzard.

Food Web. A complex energy pathway encompassing exchanges among many different species.

Geothermal Energy. Energy in the form of steam that escapes from the earth.

Greenhouse Effect. A temperature increase caused by pollutants in the air that prevent infrared, or heat, rays from bouncing back into space.

Hydrologic Cycle. The cycle in which water evaporates from oceans and inland bodies of water into the atmosphere, is returned to the earth in some form of precipitation, and eventually finds its way back to oceans and lakes.

Incineration. Burning trash. Usually some use is made of the heat produced, and material can be recovered from the ashes. Scrubbers, filters, and precipitators can remove most of the air pollutants.

Interdependence. A general ecological principle of interrelations in an ecosystem.

Natural Selection. An aspect of evolution by means of which hereditary differences that further adaptation to the particular habitat are established. The individuals that adapt best to their environment are those that survive and reproduce. Individuals lacking adaptable characteristics die out.

Niche. All the relations between any species or organism and its environment. How the organism lives, its effects upon the environment, and various environmental effects upon it constitute its ecological niche.

Nitrogen Cycle. When nitrogen in its elemental form N_2, making up 78 percent of the atmosphere, is changed through the action of bacteria and algae into nitrates (NO_3) and ammonium compounds (NH_4^+) that can be used by plants then converted into gas by denitrifying bacteria, and returned to the atmosphere as nitrogen and ammonia (NH_3).

Nitrogen Fixation. The process by which bacteria and other soil microorganisms convert atmospheric nitrogen into nitrates. Bacteria that live in the roots of legumes, alfalfa, soybeans, clover, peas, vetch, and peanuts are important in this process.

Noise. Unwanted sound.

Oligotrophic Lake. Deep, young lake, with low productivity of algae.

Particles. Bits of solid and liquid matter in the air. They include smoke, fumes, dust, and mist. New York City produces an estimated 335 tons of particulate matter on a winter day.

Persistent Pesticides. Chemical pesticides that are not biodegradable but remain in the environment for years or decades. Chlorinated hydrocarbons are one important group.

Phosphates. Chemical compounds of phosphoric acid, which are necessary to plant growth. Too much phosphate concentration in water causes rapid growth of algae, resulting in eutrophication of a body of water.

Photosynthesis. The process by which land plants, freshwater algae, and phytoplankton in the sea use sunlight energy to convert carbon dioxide and water into carbohydrates, releasing oxygen as a by-product. It is the basic process by which solar energy is converted into organic compounds.

Phytoplankton. Microscopic floating plant organisms in lakes, rivers, and oceans that supply food to higher organisms in the food chain and release oxygen as a by-product of photosynthesis. Diatoms, microscopic algae, and dinoflagellates are the principal phytoplankton of the open sea.

Pollution. A condition or process in which an ecosystem is unable to cleanse itself; the ultimate result is an upset in the balance of organisms and produces an abnormal change in the ecosystem.

Precipitator. A device used for collecting particles. An electrostatic precipitator is used to collect them from smoke.

Producer. Living green plants that supply food directly or indirectly to all higher organisms in the food web.

Pyrolysis. A destructive process in which heat is applied externally and air excluded, used for recycling of certain wastes.

Recycling. Reuse of natural and manmade resources. In natural systems all matter is constantly being recycled, though man has produced materials that cannot be recycled in reasonable periods of time.

Salt Marsh. An area of boggy, peaty ground around the borders of an estuary.

Saprovores. The final consumers in the food web; they convert dead and waste matter into carbon dioxide. Many microorganisms and fungi belong to this group.

Smog. Originally a combination of smoke and fog but now a condition of air heavily contaminated with hydrocarbons, carbon monoxide, sulfur oxides, nitrogen oxides, and particles.

Sonic Boom. A shock wave produced by an object moving through the air at speed faster than that of sound. The speed of sound in air is 770 miles an hour.

Succession. The process of changing the structure of a biological community through altering the kinds of species that inhabit it. The succession of a community may take hundreds of years.

Temperature Inversion. The abnormal atmospheric condition that occurs when a layer of cool air is trapped by a layer of warmer air above it, preventing the ground air from rising. Under normal conditions, ground air rises and is cooled as it disperses. The thermal inversion creates smog when the ground air contains pollutants.

Thermal Pollution. Raising the temperature of water above its normal level, usually by passing the water over the cooling coils of electric generators, powered either by nuclear energy or combustion of fossil fuel.

appendix a/
resource guide for environmental education in the elementary school

PROFESSIONAL BOOKS

Allen, Durward L. *Our Wildlife Legacy*. New York: Funk & Wagnalls, 1962.

Bates, Marston. *The Forest and the Sea: A Look at the Economy of Nature and the Ecology of Man*. New York: Random House, 1960.

Blake, Peter. *God's Own Junkyard: The Planned Deterioration of America's Landscape*. New York: Holt, 1964.

Borgstrom, Georg. *The Hungry Planet*. New York: Macmillan, 1965.

Bresler, J. B. *Human Ecology: Collected Readings*. Reading, Mass.: Addison-Wesley, 1966.

Burton, Maurice. *Animal Partnerships*. New York: Warne, 1970.

Caldwell, Lynton Keith. *Environment: A Challenge to Modern Society*. New York: Natural History Press, 1970.

Carr, Donald E. *The Breath of Life*. New York: Norton, 1965.

Carr, Donald E. *Death of the Sweet Waters*. New York: Norton, 1966.

Carson, Rachel. *Sense of Wonder*. New York: Harper, 1956.

Carson, Rachel. *Silent Spring*. Boston: Houghton Mifflin, 1962.

Carvajal, Joan & Martha E. Munzer. *Conservation Education: A Selected Bibliography*. Danville, Ill.: Interstate, 1968.

Clawson, Marion, R. Burnell Held & Charles H. Stoddard. *Land for the Future*. Baltimore: Johns Hopkins Press, 1960.

Cloud, Preston E., Jr. (ed.). *Resources and Man*. San Francisco: Freeman, 1969.

Commoner, Barry. *Science and Survival*. New York: Viking, 1967.

Dansereau, Pierre (ed.). *Challenge for Survival: Land, Air and Water for Man in Megalopolis*. New York: Columbia University Press, 1970.

Davies, J. Clarence, III. *The Politics of Pollution*. New York: Pegasus, 1970.

De Bell, Garrett (ed.). *The Environmental Handbook*. New York: Ballantine, 1970.

Dubos, René. *Man Adapting*. New Haven: Yale University Press, 1965.

Dubos, René. *So Human an Animal*. New York: Scribner's, 1969.

Ehrlich, Paul R. *The Population Bomb*. New York: Ballantine, 1968.

Esposito, John C. (ed.). *Vanishing Air: Ralph Nader's Study Group Report on Air Pollution*. New York: Grossman, 1970.

Fisher, Tadd. *Our Overcrowded World*. New York: Parents' Magazine Press, 1969.

Freedman, Ronald (ed.). *Population: The Vital Revolution*. New York: Anchor, 1964.

Fuller, R. Buckminister. *Operating Manual for Spaceship Earth*. Urbana: University of Illinois Press, 1968.

Gallion, Arthur B. & Simon Eisner. *The Urban Pattern: City Planning and Design*. Princeton, N.J.: Van Nostrand, 1963.

Graham, Frank, Jr. *Since Silent Spring*. Boston: Houghton Mifflin, 1970.

Gregor, Arthur. *How the World's Cities Began*. New York: Dutton, 1967.

Hardin, Garrett (ed.). *Population, Evolution and Birth Control: A Collage of Controversial Readings*. San Francisco: Freeman, 1964.

Herber, Lewis. *Crisis in Our Cities: Death, Disease and the Urban Plague*. Englewood Cliffs, N.J.: Prentice-Hall, 1965.

Herfindahl, Orris C. & Allen V. Kneese. *Quality of the Environment: An Economic Approach to Some Problems in Using Land, Water, and Air*. Baltimore: Johns Hopkins Press, 1965.

Hersh, Seymour M. *Chemical and Biological Warfare: America's Hidden Arsenal*. New York: Doubleday, 1969.

Higbee, Edward. *The Squeeze: Cities Without Space*. New York: Morrow, 1960.

Jarrett, Henry (ed.). *Perspectives on Conservation: Essays on America's Natural Resources*. Baltimore: Johns Hopkins Press, 1969.

Johnson, Huey D. (ed.). *No Deposit—No Return*. Reading, Mass.: Addison-Wesley, 1970.

Kormondy, Edward. *Concepts in Ecology*. Englewood Cliffs, N.J.: Prentice-Hall, 1969.

Kormondy, Edward. *Readings in Ecology*. Englewood Cliffs, N.J.: Prentice-Hall, 1965.

Landsberg, Hans H., Leonard L. Fischman & Joseph L. Fisher. *Resources in America's Future: Patterns of Requirements and Availabilities, 1960–2000*. Baltimore: Johns Hopkins Press, 1963.

Laycock, George. *The Diligent Destroyers*. New York: Doubleday, 1970.

Linton, Ron M. *Terracide: America's Destruction of Her Living Environment*. Boston: Little, Brown, 1970.

McClellan, Grant S. (ed.). *Protecting Our Environment*. New York: Wilson, 1970.

MacKae, Benton. *The New Exploration: A Philosophy of Regional Planning*. Urbana: University of Illinois Press, 1962.

Malthus, Thomas, Julian Huxley & Frederick Osborn. *On Population: Three Essays*. New York: New American Library, 1960.

Marx, Wesley. *The Frail Ocean*. New York: Ballantine, 1967.

Mitchell, John G. & Constance L. Stallings (eds.). *Ecotactics: The Sierra Club Handbook for Environmental Activists*. New York: Pocket Books, 1970.

Nature/Science Annual 1970: Time/Life. Morristown, N.J.: Silver Burdett, 1970.

Odum, Eugene P. *Fundamentals of Ecology*. Philadelphia: Saunders, 1959.

Paddock, William & Paul Paddock, *Famine—1975! America's Decision: Who Will Survive?* Boston: Little, Brown, 1967.

Petersen, William. *Population*. New York: Macmillan, 1961.

Reid, Keith. *Nature's Network: The Story of Ecology*. New York: Natural History Press, 1969.

Rienow, Robert & Leona Train. *Moment in the Sun*. New York: Ballantine, 1967.

Riley, Charles M. *Our Mineral Resources: An Elementary Textbook in Economic Geology*. New York: Wiley, 1959.

Rockefeller, Nelson A. *Our Environment Can Be Saved*. New York: Doubleday, 1970.

Rudd, Robert L. *Pesticides and the Living Landscape*. Madison: University of Wisconsin Press, 1964.

Smith, Frank E. *The Politics of Conservation*. New York: Random House, 1966.

Swatek, Paul. *The User's Guide to the Protection of the Environment*. New York: Ballantine, 1970.

Taylor, Gordon Rattray. *The Biological Time Bomb*. New York: World, 1968.

Tietze, Frederick I. & James E. McKeown (eds.). *The Changing Metropolis*. Boston: Houghton Mifflin, 1964.

Udall, Stewart. *1976: Agenda for Tomorrow*. New York: Harcourt, 1968.

Udall, Stewart L. *The Quiet Crisis*. New York: Holt, 1963.

Von Eckardt, Wolf. *The Challenge of Megalopolis: A Graphic Presentation of the Urbanized Northeastern Seaboard of the United States*. New York: Macmillan, 1964.

Waters, John F. *The Sea Farmers*. New York: Hastings, 1970.

Ziswiler, Vinzeny. *Extinct and Vanishing Animals: A Biology of Extinction and Survival*. New York: Springer, 1967.

CURRICULUM GUIDES

Act in Time. Indiana State Department of Public Instruction, Division of Curriculum, Room 108, State Office Building, Indianapolis 46204. 1969. Art and environmental education. Kindergarten through twelfth grade.

Audubon Nature Bulletin 2: 14 Good Teaching Aids. National Audubon Society, 1130 Fifth Avenue, New York, New York 10028. Covers a wide range of subjects and activities in natural science.

Checklist of Educational Environments Desirable on School-Controlled Property, by John Brainerd. The Nature Conservancy, 1522 K Street, N.W., Washington, D.C. 20005.

Classroom Out-of-Doors, by Wilbur Schramm. Sequoia Press, Publishers, 300 West Kalamazoo, Kalamazoo, Michigan 49006. 1969.

Curriculum Outline for Elementary and Secondary Schools in Oceanography and Marine Biology. Oceanography Unlimited, 108 Main Street, Lodi, New Jersey 07644. 1969.

Developing a Marine Science Program. Oceanography Unlimited, 108 Main Street, Lodi, New Jersey 07644. 1969.

Environmental Education Instruction Plans. Conservation and Environmental Science Center, 5400 Glenwood Avenue, Minneapolis, Minnesota 55422. 1969. Ten plans.

Environmental Education—Objectives and Field Activities, by Major, Cissell, and others. Paducah Public Schools, Environmental Education, 10th and Clark Streets, P.O. Box 1137, Paducah, Kentucky 42001. Outdoor-education curriculum guide, including activities, and experiments; interdisciplinary. Kindergarten through twelfth grade. 1969.

Experiments with Living Things, by Vessel and Applegarth. Fearon Publishers, 2165 Park Boulevard, Palo Alto, California 94306. Guides for working in the field.

Forest and Teacher's Guide. Fernbank Science Center, 156 Heaton Park Drive N.W., Atlanta, Georgia 30307. Kindergarten through twelfth grade.

The Forest Is a Classroom, by the Minnesota News Service. The Nature Conservancy, 1522 K Street, N.W., Washington, D.C. 20005. 1969. How to set up a natural area for teaching.

Guidelines for Environmental Sensitivity, by Eleanor Bennett et al. Pennsylvania Department of Education, Commonwealth of Pennsylvania, Harrisburg, Pennsylvania 17126. 1969. Kindergarten through twelfth grade.

Man and His Environment: An Introduction to Using Environmental Study Areas, by the Association of Classroom Teachers. National Education Association, 1201 Sixteenth Street, N.W., Washington, D.C. 20036. 1970.

Our Precarious Habitat, by Melvin A. Benarge. W. W. Norton & Company, 55 Fifth Avenue, New York, New York 10003. Complex interactions in the environment.

People and Their Environment: Teachers' Curriculum Guides to Conservation Education, ed. by Matthew J. Brennan. J. G. Ferguson Publishing Co., 6 North Michigan Avenue, Chicago, Illinois 60602. 1969. Eight volumes.

School Site Development for Conservation and Outdoor Education, by Eleanor Bennett. Pennsylvania Department of Education, Commonwealth of Pennsylvania, Harrisburg, Pennsylvania 17126. 1969. Interdisciplinary. Kindergarten through twelfth grade.

Science Skilltexts, by Neal and Perkins. Charles E. Merrill Publishing Co., 1300 Alum Creek Drive, Columbus, Ohio 43216. 1966. Conservation and pollution, activities and experiments. Elementary grades.

Teachers Guide for Environmental Education. The Task Force on Environment and Natural Resources, The North Carolina Department of Public Instruction, Raleigh, North Carolina. 1970.

FILMS AND FILMSTRIPS

Contemporary Films (distributor), 267 West 25th Street, New York, New York 10001. *Silent Spring of Rachel Carson,* produced by CBS.

Coronet Films, 65 E. South Water Street, Chicago, Illinois 60601. *How Insects Help Us* and *How Plants Help Us.*

Department of Interior, Conservation Education Department, Peachtree-7th Building, Atlanta, Georgia 30323. *The River Must Live* (21 minutes).

Ealing Corporation, Film Loops, 2225 Massachusetts Avenue, Cambridge, Massachusetts 02140. Titles include (in sets) *The Undersea World of Jacques Cousteau* (13 loops), *The Changing City* (9 loops), *Habitats* (4 loops), and others. Individual loops include "Flash Flood," "A Volcano in Action," and "Geographic Causes of Deserts." Encyclopaedia Britannica Films, 38 W. 32nd Street, New York, New York 10001. *Pond Life, This Vital Earth* (Living Earth Series), *Balanced Aquarium* (11 minutes, color), and *A Tree Is a Living Thing* (11 minutes, color).

Imperial Film Co., 321 South Florida Avenue, Lakeland, Florida 33802. *Ecological Systems,* a filmstrip and record.

Jam Handy School Service Center, Scott Education Division, 2781 East Grand Boulevard, Detroit, Michigan 48211. *Adventures in Nature* includes 9 filmstrips, such as "A Walk in the Woods," "A Walk Around a Pond," and "A Walk in the City." Other sets include *Plant Structure and Growth* and *Insect Societies.*

Life Education Program, Box 834, Radio City Post Office, New York, New York 10019. Pollution series of filmstrips including Part I: *The Great Lakes: History and Ecology,* Part II: *The Great Lakes: The Causes of Pollution,* and Part III: *The Great Lakes: The Results of Pollution.*

McGraw-Hill Films, 330 West 42nd Street, New York, New York 10036. Sixty films on the environment, conservation, and pollution are available, including *Air Pollution: Take a Deep Deadly Breath, Tomorrow's World: Feeding the Billions, The Problem with Water Is People, The World Around Us, The Silent Spring of Rachel Carson,* and *Poisons, Pests and People.*

New York State Air Pollution Control Board, 84 Holland Avenue, Albany, New York 12208. *With Each Breath.*

Popular Science Audio-Visuals, 5235 Ravenswood Avenue, Chicago, Illinois 60640. Filmstrip titles include *Ecology and Conservation* (series), *Ecology—Interdependence* (series), "Air Pollution," and "The Problem of Air Pollution."

U.S. Public Health Service, Welfare Building, Fifth Street and Independence Avenue, S.W., Washington, D.C. 20201. Publication No. 1264 describes free films on air pollution that can be ordered from the U.S. Government Printing Office, Washington, D.C. 20402. Price of booklet 15 cents. Sixteen sixteen-millimeter films and two thirty-five-millimeter filmstrips ("Sources of Air Pollution" and "Effects of Air Pollution") are available.

Walt Disney Productions, Educational Film Division, 350 South Buena Vista

Avenue, Burbank, California 91503. *Nature's Half Acre* (True Life Adventures Series).

Ward's Educational Filmstrips, Ward's Natural Science Establishment, Inc., P.O. Box 1712, Rochester, New York 12603; or P.O. Box 1749, Monterey, California 93940, *Environmental Pollution*, series of six filmstrips covering air, water, and land pollution.

KITS, GAMES, SIMULATIONS, AND RELATED AIDS

Audubon Ecology Chart. National Audubon Society, 1130 Fifth Avenue, New York, New York 10028. 1966. Colored map of North America, showing the principal biomes, with paintings of the principal plants and animals of each.

Conservation Teaching Aids, Kellogg Bird Sanctuary, Route 1, Box 339, Augusta, Michigan 49012. Wall charts, notebook charts, leaflets, slide-tape programs, overhead-projection series.

How a Tree Grows. U.S. Government Printing Office, Washington, D.C. 20402. 1968. Poster.

Kits for Science. Stephen Rituper, Jr., Bethlehem Area School District, 1330 Church Street, Bethlehem, Pennsylvania 18015. 1970. Ungraded individualized taped kits. Titles include *Awareness of Heat Pollution, Factory Heat and Water, and Factory Heat and Air.*

Laboratory Exercises in Marine Science, ed. by S. Lavene. Martin County High School, Stuart, Florida 33494. 1970.

Nature Study Aids, Conservation Education, Red Wing, Minnesota 55066. NASCO Nature Study Aids. Series of visual aids and student activities, including exact replicas of leaves, plant structures, and the feet of wild animals from our environment.

Synopsis of Games and Simulations in ERCA Life Science, by Fred A. Rasmussen. Educational Research Council of America, Rockefeller Building, Cleveland, Ohio 44113. 1969. Interdisciplinary approach. One game is "the pollution game."

3 M Company, Visual Products Division, 3 M Center, St. Paul, Minnesota 55101. Color Transparencies, including "The Land that Supports Us," "Our Soil Resources," "Our Water Resources," "Our Plant Resources," "Our Animal Resources."

Wall charts on pond life, oceanography, seeds, and ecology. Grade Teacher Reprints, 23 Leroy Ave., Darien, Connecticut 06820. 1967-1969. Kindergarten through sixth grade.

ORGANIZATIONS CONCERNED WITH THE ENVIRONMENT

American Forestry Association
919 Seventeenth Street N.W.
Washington, D.C. 20006

Animal Welfare Institute
>   P.O. Box 3492
>   Grand Central Station
>   New York, New York 10017
>   Has a valuable publication available on use and care of animals in the classroom.

Association for Voluntary Sterilization
>   14 West 40th Street
>   New York, New York 10018

Environmental Defense Fund
>   P.O. Drawer 740
>   Stony Brook, New York 11790
>   A national coalition of scientists, lawyers, and citizens who are fighting encroachments upon the environment through legal means.

Friends of the Earth
>   30 East 42nd Street
>   New York, New York 10017

Hugh Moore Fund
>   60 East 42nd Street
>   New York, New York 10017
>   Concerned with population control; supports organizations with similar interests.

Izaak Walton League
>   1326 Waukegan Road
>   Glenview, Illinois 60025

League of Women Voters
>   1730 M Street N.W.
>   Washington, D.C. 20036

National Audubon Society
>   1130 Fifth Avenue
>   New York, New York 10028
>   Members are entitled to *Audubon*, a bimonthly publication containing beautifully illustrated and timely articles on nature topics. *Audubon Ecology Chart* and *Audubon Study Guides* and many other teaching aids are available.

National Geographic Society
>   17th and M Streets N.W.
>   Washington, D.C. 20036
>   Members receive *National Geographic* monthly.

National Parks Association
>   Washington, D.C. 20009
>   Publishes *National Parks* monthly and maintains a conservation library.

National Wildlife Federation
>   1412 Sixteenth Street N.W.
>   Washington, D.C. 20036
>   Publishes *National Wildlife* bimonthly and *Ranger Rick* for elementary-school children.

The Nature Conservancy
      1522 K Street N.W.
      Washington, D.C. 20005
Planned Parenthood-World Population
      515 Madison Avenue
      New York, New York 10022
      Has 188 affiliates with 524 clinics in the United States; conducts educational and promotional activities.
Population Reference Bureau
      1755 Massachusetts Avenue, N.W.
      Washington, D.C. 20036
Sierra Club
      1050 Mills Tower
      San Francisco, California 94104
The Wilderness Society
      729 Fifteenth Street N.W.
      Washington, D.C. 20005
      Sponsors wilderness trips open to all.
Zero Population Growth
      367 State Street
      Los Altos, California 94022
      A recently formed organization that intends to use political action in dealing with environmental problems.
Tuberculosis and Respiratory Disease Association
      National Headquarters
      1740 Broadway
      New York, New York 10019
      Has many local chapters.

appendix b/
/phosphates in detergents

Much confusion has arisen over the phosphorus content in laundry detergents. Phosphorus not only cleans clothes; it also helps to convert the country's lakes and streams into reservoirs of algae, resulting in eutrophication of bodies of water.

Consumers Union has listed each detergent brand's pollution potential per single wash or dishwasher load. The "amount used" is the minimum amount recommended on the package label for a top-loading machine or dishwasher. (Please keep in mind that pressures on the detergent industry will undoubtedly bring changes in these measurements. These data reflect the situation in mid-1970.)

Laundry Detergents	Amount Used (in Cups)	Phosphate per Load (in Grams)
Cold Water All (liquid)	½	0
Duz Soap	1½	0
Ivory Flakes	1½	0
Lux Flakes	1½	0
Sears Enzyme Laundry Detergent	½	0*
Whirlpool Laundry Detergent	½	0*
A & P White Sail	†	2
Jet Power	½	9
Amway S-A-8	¼	16
Easy Bright	1	17
Fyne Tex	1	17
Grand	1	17
Key Food	1	17
Pathmark All Purpose Detergent	1	17
Shop Rite All Purpose Detergent	1	17

Laundry Detergents (*cont.*)	Amount Used (in Cups)	Phosphate per Load (in Grams)
Staff	1	17
Wisk	½	17
Hudso	½	18
Pathmark Cold Water Detergent	1	18
Service Soft	½	18
Shop Rite Cold Water Detergent	1	18
Market Basket Blue	1½	23
Shopping Bag	1½	23
Vons	1½	25
Brillo Detergent	1¼	26
Cheer	1¼	26
News Detergent	1¼	26
Gain	1¼	26
Lucky Low Suds	¾	27
O-So-Kleen	¾	27
Stater Bros.	¾	27
Rinso	1¼	28
Bio-Ad	1¼	29
Bold	1¼	29
Cold Power	1¼	29
Dreft	1½	29
Fab	1¼	29
Farm Service Laundry Detergent	1	30
Food Giant	1½	30
Sears Enzyme Laundry Detergent	½	30
Surf	1¼	30
Ajax Laundry	1¼	31
Bonus	1½	32
Punch	1¼	32
Silver Dust	1¼	33
Duz Detergent	1½	34
Oxydol	1¼	34
Breeze	2	41
Drive	1¼	41
Cold Water All (powder)	1¼	42
Concentrated All	1	42
Tide XK	1¼	43‡
Dash	¾	47
Salvo	§	47
A & P Blue Sail	1½	48

Presoaks	Amount Used (in Cups)	Phosphate per Load (in Grams)
Amway Tri-zyme	½	13
Brion	½	19
Sears Enzyme Presoak	½	22
Axion	½	34
Biz	½	34

Automatic Dishwashing Detergents	Amount Used (in Tablespoons)	Phosphate per Load (in Grams)
Electrasol (soft water)	1½	4
Finish	1½	4.3
Electrasol (hard water)	1½	6
Sears Automatic	1½	6.6
Finish (medium water)	1½	6.9
Amway	2	8.3
Calgonite	2	8.5
All	2	9.8
Finish (hard water)	1½	10
Cascade	2½	12

This list is taken from "Dead Lakes: Another Washday Miracle," *Consumer Reports*, September 1970. Reprinted by permission. The publisher, Consumers Union, wishes to stress that the material is now dated and, further, that the pressures on the industry for change will undoubtedly eventually make the material outdated.
* As of August 15, 1970.
† A "good squeeze."
‡ Only 75 percent of this figure for about ⅓ of present production.
§ Two tablets.

index

A

Abstract community, 29
Activity sequence, 30
Administrative aides, 54
Affective learning, 49, 169–173
Air pollution, 84–86
  and smoking and lung cancer,
    138–139
Air travel, 152
Alaskan oil pipeline, 106–107
Alexander, A. S., 157
Alexander, W. M., 24
Allen, J. E., Jr., 18
Alston, R. E., 37, 39
Animals, population control in,
    130–132
Anthropology, and environmental
    education, 66
Ardrey, R., 131
Arena, J. E., 59
Association for Supervision and
    Curriculum Development, 8–9
Autecologist, 24
Autotrophic organisms, 32
Ayers, T. L., 72

B

Bach, G. L., 34
Bakan, R., 134
Baker, E. I., 45, 58
Baker, P. T., 66
Baldwin, A. L., 58
Bauer, N. W., 171–172
Behavioral goals, 46–48
Benton, A. H., 37
Binomial nomenclature, 36
Biomedical research, 9–10
Biomes, 27
Biotic community, 118–119
Biotic province, 29
Birth control, 9
Blackaby, F., 157
Blokhin, N., 138
Bloom, B. S., 48
Bloomfield, H., 107
Borgstrom, G., 133
Boyer, W. H., 176
Brandwein, P. F., 7–8, 19, 69, 78
Breder, C. M., Jr., 141
Brennan, M. J., 69, 78
Breysse, P. A., 93